Cambridge Elements

Elements in the Philosophy of Biology
edited by
Grant Ramsey
KU Leuven

HEALTH AND DISEASE

Experimental Philosophy of Medicine

Somogy Varga
Aarhus University

Andrew James Latham
Aarhus University

Edouard Machery
University of Pittsburgh

Shaftesbury Road, Cambridge CB2 8EA, United Kingdom

One Liberty Plaza, 20th Floor, New York, NY 10006, USA

477 Williamstown Road, Port Melbourne, VIC 3207, Australia

314–321, 3rd Floor, Plot 3, Splendor Forum, Jasola District Centre, New Delhi – 110025, India

103 Penang Road, #05–06/07, Visioncrest Commercial, Singapore 238467

Cambridge University Press is part of Cambridge University Press & Assessment, a department of the University of Cambridge.

We share the University's mission to contribute to society through the pursuit of education, learning and research at the highest international levels of excellence.

www.cambridge.org
Information on this title: www.cambridge.org/9781009673716

DOI: 10.1017/9781009673679

© Somogy Varga, Andrew James Latham, and Edouard Machery 2026

This publication is in copyright. Subject to statutory exception and to the provisions of relevant collective licensing agreements, no reproduction of any part may take place without the written permission of Cambridge University Press & Assessment.

When citing this work, please include a reference to the DOI 10.1017/9781009673679

First published 2026

A catalogue record for this publication is available from the British Library

A Cataloging-in-Publication data record for this Element is available from the Library of Congress

ISBN 978-1-009-67370-9 Hardback
ISBN 978-1-009-67371-6 Paperback
ISSN 2515-1126 (online)
ISSN 2515-1118 (print)

Cambridge University Press & Assessment has no responsibility for the persistence or accuracy of URLs for external or third-party internet websites referred to in this publication and does not guarantee that any content on such websites is, or will remain, accurate or appropriate.

For EU product safety concerns, contact us at Calle de José Abascal, 56, 1°, 28003 Madrid, Spain, or email eugpsr@cambridge.org

Health and Disease

Experimental Philosophy of Medicine

Elements in the Philosophy of Biology

DOI: 10.1017/9781009673679
First published online: January 2026

Somogy Varga
Aarhus University

Andrew J. Latham
Aarhus University

Edouard Machery
University of Pittsburgh

Author for correspondence: Somogy Varga, varga@cas.au.dk

Abstract: The concepts of health and disease are fundamental to medical research, healthcare, and public health, and philosophers have long sought to clarify their meaning and implications. Increasingly, it is suggested that progress in this area could be advanced by integrating empirical methods with philosophical reflection. This Element explores the emerging field of experimental philosophy of medicine (XPhiMed), which takes this approach by applying empirical methods to longstanding philosophical debates. It begins with an overview of the philosophical debates and their methodological challenges, followed by an exploration of experimental findings on health, disease, and disorder, along with their implications for philosophy and other fields.

Keywords: Health, disease, experimental philosophy, dysfunction, medicine

© Somogy Varga, Andrew James Latham, and Edouard Machery 2026

ISBNs: 9781009673709 (HB), 9781009673716 (PB), 9781009673679 (OC)
ISSNs: 2515-1126 (online), 2515-1118 (print)

Contents

0 Brief Introduction — 1

1 Philosophy of Health and Disease: Issues and Methods — 2

2 Health — 23

3 Disease and Dysfunction — 42

4 XPhiMed: Insights and Future Prospects — 57

   Bibliography — 64

0 Brief Introduction

Just like many other major fields, medicine is accompanied by a philosophical subdiscipline – philosophy of medicine – that examines the epistemological, metaphysical, and methodological aspects of medicine. Over the last fifty years, debates over the concepts of disease and health have emerged as pivotal issues, gaining prominence in part due to their profound implications for both the medical field and society at large (for reviews, see Kingma 2019; Murphy 2021). Clarifying these concepts is crucial for medical research, healthcare, and public health as the categorization of conditions based on these concepts can influence treatment options, research priorities, legal rights, social perceptions, and the allocation of scarce resources. Moreover, as medicine can often appear to encroach beyond its traditional boundaries, the concepts of health and disease have also become important in debates about what legitimately falls within the scope of medicine (Stegenga 2018; Varga 2024). This ongoing expansion and the critical discourse surrounding it underscore the need for a nuanced understanding of these concepts.

Despite the importance of this matter and longstanding philosophical interest, many philosophers have grown pessimistic about making any further philosophical progress, citing methodological constraints that have seemingly brought these discussions to an impasse (Lemoine 2013; Sholl 2015; Schwartz 2017; Fuller 2018). There is a growing sentiment that to advance philosophical debates on health and disease, it is important to incorporate new methodologies, including empirical approaches like those used in experimental philosophy (Griffiths and Stotz 2008; De Block and Hens 2021; Faucher 2021; Faucher and Béghin 2023).

This Element aims to do just this by showcasing how the empirical methods from experimental philosophy are useful to clarify the concepts of health and disease. More generally, this Element systematically explores the emerging field of *experimental philosophy of medicine* (XPhiMed), bridging traditional philosophical approaches with cutting-edge empirical research.

The Element starts with an overview of the philosophical debates about health and disease (Section 1). This section highlights the methodological limitations of traditional approaches as well as the importance of experimental methodologies, while drawing parallels to empirical research from sociology, anthropology, and health psychology. The following sections then systematically explore experimental philosophy's findings about the concept of health (Section 2) as well as about the concepts of disease and disorder (Section 3). Section 2 examines in particular whether physical or mental health is understood as merely the absence of diseases or disorders. Section 3 turns to the concepts of disease and disorder and examines the role of biological dysfunction and people's evaluations of a condition in disease and disorder ascriptions.

We are grateful to the following colleagues for their comments on previous drafts of this Element: Daian Flórez, Eric Hochstein, Carl Hoefer, Lucy James, Richard Samuels, Aliya Rumana, Eric Snyder, and Hein van den Berg for comments on Section 1 at the weekly reading group of the Center for Philosophy of Science at the University of Pittsburgh in September 2024; Alexandre Billon, Nora Hangel, Carl Hoefer, Frédéric Jaeck, Lucy James, Mahdi Khalili, Andrea Roselli, and Aliya Rumana for comments on Section 2 at the weekly reading group of the Center for Philosophy of Science at the University of Pittsburgh in March 2025.

1 Philosophy of Health and Disease: Issues and Methods

The longstanding philosophical debate over the concepts of health and disease has spawned a multitude of positions, and there are numerous ways to describe and systematize them. For our purposes, we will refer to the main issues as the *evaluative issue* (whether the concepts of health and disease are evaluative or nonevaluative) and the *relational issue* (how the concepts of health and disease are related to each other). To set the stage for a more comprehensive exploration, here is a snapshot of these two central issues and the primary positions in the philosophical literature. There are three main positions concerning the evaluative issue: *naturalism*, which holds that the concepts of disease and health are nonevaluative concepts, *normativism*, which claims that they are evaluative concepts, and *hybridism*, which claims that the concepts of disease and health have both nonevaluative and evaluative elements. There are two main positions concerning the relational issue: *negativism* maintains that health is the absence of disease, whereas *positivism* maintains that health is not (or not just) the absence of disease, but rather involves the presence of some distinct condition.

It is rarely clear whether the theories we will be discussing below are intended to be theories of health and disease *themselves* or of the *concepts* of health and disease. The two, of course, can differ substantially: if we wanted to know what water is, we would ask chemists and we would be told that it is a substance made of molecules of H_2O (to simplify a more complicated story); if we wanted to know what the concept of water is, we would ask psychologists, philosophers, or linguists and we would perhaps be told that people think of water as the stuff that fills seas and lakes, falls from the sky as rain, satisfies our thirst, and so on. Philosophers of medicine, we suspect, often care about developing theories of health and disease *themselves* but also believe, more or less explicitly, that the way to develop a theory of health and disease is to develop a theory of the *concepts* of health and disease. They embrace, often implicitly, a form of conceptual analysis (see Fagerberg 2023 for a critical discussion), in which by analyzing the concept of something we learn what a thing must be. To wit, they often move seamlessly from claims about what diseases or health are, to claims about the concepts of health and disease. Boorse (1977) intends to tell us what a disease is when he writes that "A disease is a type of internal state which impairs health, i.e., reduces one or more functional abilities below typical efficiency" (p. 555), but refers throughout to the concept of disease (indeed, his famous 1977 paper is called "health as a theoretical concept"). Cooper (2002) tells us that "someone who has a disease is unlucky," (p. 276; see below), but also discusses "the *concept* of disorder" (our emphasis). Below we follow philosophers of medicine in moving from diseases and health to their concepts, and we draw the distinction between diseases or health and their concepts only when it matters.

Before offering a more detailed discussion, three points need emphasis. First, it is beneficial to address the evaluative and relational issues separately, as these represent conceptually distinct questions. While naturalism is commonly associated with negativism, and normativism with positivism, there are notable exceptions (e.g., Cooper 2002, 2005, 2020). Second, adopting a certain position about health and disease does not require holding the same view regarding particular diseases. For instance, normativists are free to think that distinctions *between* diseases solely depend on psychological and biological facts (Giroux 2016). Third, it is often overlooked in the debate about health and disease that the accounts presented by the main protagonists vary, explicitly or implicitly, in their scope. We find it helpful to distinguish between *restricted accounts* and *unrestricted accounts*. Unrestricted accounts, which include most positions in the literature, are intended to apply to both lay and technical concepts of health and disease (e.g., Reznek 1987; Wakefield 1992a, 2007; Cooper 2002). In contrast, restricted accounts are only meant to apply to the concept of health as it is used in technical context such as medical practice or theory, though not necessarily to the lay concept of health. For instance, Boorse accepts that terms like "illness" are value-laden in both lay use and medical practice, and he acknowledges that the purely descriptive concept has to be augmented with values in order to be relevant for treatment or policy, but he insists that his analysis focuses on the theoretical use of "disease" (Boorse 1975, 55; 1997; 2011; 2014).

1.1 The Evaluative Issue

Naturalism

Proponents of naturalism argue that health and disease can be understood in purely descriptive terms, as these proponents characterize diseases as grounded in objective natural categories of biological function and dysfunction, which are independent of evaluative considerations. Naturalism is often viewed as appealing because it is perceived as providing (a) a potential safeguard against overmedicalization (roughly the problematic tendency to categorize various conditions as medical issues) and (b) objective support in resolving debates about what constitutes health or disease, which could otherwise be mired in profound value-based disagreements. Boorse's Bio-Statistical Theory (1975, 1976, 1977, 1997, 2014) is a sophisticated and influential naturalist approach, shaping debates not only in the philosophy of medicine but also about ethical aspects of healthcare and distributive justice.

The Bio-Statistical Theory characterizes the human organism as being composed of numerous subsystems, each of which has a biological function. While some accounts define biological function in evolutionary terms as the effect for which a trait was naturally selected, the Bio-Statistical Theory comprehends them in terms of its species-typical causal contribution to the survival and reproduction of the organism. The unit of comparison with respect to which the species-typicality of a contribution is determined is the "reference class" – a unit consisting of the individuals who belong to the same age group and sex (Boorse 1977, 555; 2014). A disease is a condition that results in the failure of a subsystem or part to perform its biological function. It is thus causally associated with a "dysfunction." On the Bio-Statistical Theory, "disease" and "pathological condition" are to a large extent interchangeable, and refer to "a type of internal state which impairs health, i.e., reduces one or more functional abilities below typical efficiency" (Boorse 2014, 684). They differ from "illness," whose meaning is partly evaluative. Health is simply the absence of disease, and thus is species-typical functioning, defined as the statistically representative contribution of the organs and parts of the organism to survival and reproduction (Boorse 2014).

Overall, then, the Bio-Statistical Theory describes diseases and disorders in terms of departures from natural norms (as opposed to social norms), as deviations from the proper physiological or psychological function of parts of the human organism. For this reason, as Boorse (1997, 4) puts it, "the classification of human states as healthy or diseased can be read off the biological facts of nature."

While this is not the place to consider the entire range of criticism and the defenses Boorse has mounted over the years, the Bio-Statistical Theory has been criticized for ultimately providing a value-laden analysis (Fulford 1989; Murphy 2006; Ereshefsky 2009; Barnes 2023), and for being unable to account for counterexamples in medical literature (DeVito 2000; Guerrero 2010; Kingma 2010). It is, however, worth considering one influential line of criticism. This concerns the Bio-Statistical Theory's selection of age and sex as the criteria for defining reference classes. Critics argue that there is no principled rationale for designating age and sex as the defining parameters for reference classes, while excluding other candidates such as race, sexual orientation, or socioeconomic status (Cooper 2005; Kingma 2007, 2013; Schwartz 2007a).

Other naturalist approaches often build on the Bio-Statistical Theory while attempting to address some of the criticisms leveled against it. For example, Daniel Hausman (2012, 2015) grants that his own account could be seen more as a reinterpretation of the Bio-Statistical Theory rather than an alternative (2012, 520). First, while Boorse identifies functions with the typical contribution of a part or a process to "survival and reproduction," what matters for Hausman is the contribution to some goal, survival, *or* reproduction, *or* possibly something else. Second, Hausman rejects Boorse's emphasis on statistical prevalence in determining what counts as disease and dysfunction, arguing that "levels of functioning that threaten system goals...will be pathological, regardless of their frequency" (Hausman 2014, 645): on his view, even when diseases become so widespread in a population that they appear statistically normal, they are still diseases. Finally, he addresses what he sees as a problem in Boorse's account: that normal functioning in abnormal or harmful environments could be wrongly classified as healthy, since Boorse defines health solely in terms of statistically normal functioning within a reference class. Instead, Hausman proposes indexing the assessment of health and disease to "benchmark environments" – roughly, common, stable conditions in which the relevant organism typically thrives and where the part or process makes a difference (Hausman 2012, 2015). As a result, Hausman maintains that normal functioning in a harmful or abnormal environment would not count as healthy, as it might under Boorse's account. The effectiveness of these modifications in addressing the main lines of criticism against Boorse remains debated (Kingma 2017; Barnes 2023).

A final additional point about naturalism is that the accounts described here primarily focus on analyzing the theoretical concepts of health and disease. These accounts regard the medical profession's usage, rather than lay usage, as authoritative concerning these concepts' content.

Normativism

The basic difference between normativism and naturalism is helpfully illustrated by Kingma (2014, 593) with the case of infertility. As opposed to naturalists, normativists hold that "labeling wanted infertility a disease, even in theory, makes a mistake: it fails to identify the correct unifying feature that diseases share." This unifying feature that determines whether a condition is a disease is not dysfunction, but some *evaluative* content like being bad, harmful, or unwanted, or requiring medical intervention (e.g., Fulford 1989; Cooper 2002, 2020).

Some normativists emphasize that health and disease are fundamentally connected to human values and interests. According to them, the concept of illness originated from the strong negative value assigned to conditions such as pain, discomfort, and incapacity, leading to a therapeutic focus on these conditions. As medical science progressed, it began to identify conditions it called "diseases" and "dysfunctions" as the underlying causes, but the concepts of disease and dysfunction remained rooted in the notion of illness, with their content shaped by these initial practical concerns (Goosens 1980; Fulford 1989). Other views suggest that labeling a condition as a disease (rather than fatigue, demonic possession, or a moral flaw) not only describes a condition, but also implicitly mandates medical intervention or at least determines certain social obligations and entitlements. The concept of disease is thus intertwined with ethical and normative concepts (e.g., Engelhardt 1976; Goosens 1980; for discussion, see Giroux 2016).

Among normativist positions, Cooper's (2002) tripartite account is well known. Starting from the assumption that a disease is inherently undesirable, she proposes three individually necessary and collectively sufficient conditions for something to be a disease: A condition is a disease if and only if it (1) is a bad thing to have, (2) is such that we consider the person with the condition unlucky, and (3) can potentially be medically treated (Cooper 2002, 271).

Criterion (3) separates diseases from other bad and unfortunate states that meet criteria (1) and (2), but that clearly do not qualify as diseases like being extremely poor or a victim of a natural disaster. Criterion (2) separates disease from other non-diseases that might meet criteria (1).

For example, it might be bad for humans that we age or that our sense of smell is inferior to that of many animals, but aging and a poor sense of smell are not diseases. Moreover, it specifies that a condition can only be a disease if the person having it is "unlucky as judged by the uninformed layman, that is, roughly, worse off than the majority of humans of the same sex and age" (Cooper 2002, 276). Certainly, these criteria are not without challenges (see, e.g., Smart 2016). For example, if we define "disease" in terms of what medicine could potentially treat, then the boundaries of disease will shift as medical goals and technologies evolve. But it seems counterintuitive to let our concept of disease be so fluid, changing simply because medicine's capabilities or goals change. Also, the definition of "unlucky" as being worse off than most in the same sex and age group seems inconsistent with the existence of diseases that are relatively common in old age groups. Further, the choice of age and sex to characterize the contrast class invites criticisms similar to those affecting Boorse's Bio-Statistical Theory.

Crucially, criterion (1) specifies that for a condition to be classified as a disease, it must negatively impact the person experiencing it. This assessment is based on the individual's personal experience, rather than society's broader view of the condition as being undesirable (2002, 274–275). A condition can thus be bad, and thus a disease for one individual, but not for another. Cooper illustrates this point with the example of sterility: while an individual who opts for a vasectomy will no longer have a functioning reproductive system, this condition is not deemed a disease; this very condition is however a disease for someone who desires children but is involuntarily sterile. Critics have objected to the idea that a condition can oscillate between being a disease or not being a disease based solely on an individual's goals and values: it seems strange that someone changing their goals and values not only modifies whether a condition is bad for them, but also can turn this condition from being disease to being healthy or vice versa.

Other normativists focus on health and derive its normative significance from its connection to well-being either by (1) positing that health is a kind of well-being or by (2) positing a constitutive relationship between health and well-being.

The first, stronger position simply identifies health with well-being or with a kind of well-being. A prominent example is the World Health Organization's definition of health that was introduced in 1948 and remains in its constitution today. According to this definition, health is "a state of complete physical, mental and social well-being and not merely the absence of disease or infirmity" (World Health Organization 1948, 100; for discussion, see Schramme 2023). This approach can be criticized for neglecting the distinction between health and well-being. If health were simply identical to well-being, then it would be mysterious how people can prioritize well-being at the expense of health. Additionally, any decrease in health would necessarily imply a decrease in well-being, and vice versa, but there are numerous instances, such as prostate cancer in older men, where a disease is present without any unpleasant symptoms and thus without affecting well-being; furthermore, improving health by treating the condition does not guarantee an enhancement in well-being.

The second, weaker position maintains that health is important for well-being and that disease or pathology (illness, disease, injury, etc.) is bad for us insofar as it detracts from our overall well-being. On Nordenfelt's (1995, 2007) account, health amounts to the possession of certain abilities that are required for pursuing "vital goals," the satisfaction of which is necessary and jointly sufficient for achieving "minimal happiness." For Nordenfelt, health consists in having second-order abilities to obtain those first-order abilities that are necessary to achieve these vital goals. Thus, a person with severe dyslexia is in poor health on this account because acquiring the ability to read, itself an ability, is necessary to fulfill vital goals in some contemporary social contexts and is challenging for her. Of course, people can be unable to fulfill vital goals for a number of circumstances distinct from poor health. For instance, poverty can prevent people from acquiring reading skills.

According to Nordenfelt, which goals count as "vital" is a matter of individual subjective preferences, but not all goals can count as vital: someone who has a very ambitious goal (e.g., winning the Olympics) but who, despite access to the best training, never masters the required ability to achieve that goal would hardly count as lacking health (Schramme 2007). So Nordenfelt restricts the notion of vital goals to the ones the satisfaction of which is necessary to have a very basic level of subjective quality of life across the lifespan. But then his account would suggest that people with life-threatening but perhaps relatively asymptomatic diseases, that intuitively compromise health, are in fact healthy, provided that they have the capacity to pursue the basic goods necessary to experience normal levels of basic life satisfaction.

Venkatapuram (2011, 2013) also views health as a second-order ability to attain capabilities essential for well-being, but, unlike Nordenfelt, he does not link health to an agent's personal goals and their satisfaction. Instead, he opts for an objectivist theory, arguing that health is best seen as the "metacapability" to achieve the set of fundamental human capabilities and goods described by Martha Nussbaum. These include nourishment, shelter, and meaningful relationships, which are seen as necessary for well-being, whether or not an individual desires them or is motivated to pursue them. As Venkatapuram puts it, this "metacapability" enables the obtainment of "a cluster of basic capabilities to be and do things that reflect a life worthy of equal human dignity" (2011, 71). While this objectivist approach addresses certain weaknesses in Nordenfelt's account, one might argue that health as a "metacapability" results in an overly broad account that fails to clearly separate health from other capabilities or enabling social conditions, such as education, legal protections, or income (Richardson 2016).

Hybridism

Hybrid accounts suggest that the concept of disease comprises both a non-evaluative and an evaluative component (Matthewson and Griffiths 2017; Stegenga 2018). Each component is necessary, and when combined, they are jointly sufficient for something to count as a disease.

Wakefield's influential harmful dysfunction analysis is concerned with the concept of mental disorder (Wakefield 1992a, 1992b, 2007), but his account applies to physical diseases as well (1999, 376). On the harmful dysfunction analysis, a condition counts as a disorder if and only if

> (a) the condition causes some harm or deprivation of benefit to the person as judged by the standards of the person's culture (the value criterion), and (b) the condition results from the inability of some internal mechanism to perform its natural function, wherein a natural function is an effect that is part of the evolutionary explanation of the existence and structure of the mechanism (the explanatory criterion) (Wakefield 1992a, 384).

The dysfunction component of this account is reminiscent of Boorse's analysis, who also defines disease as biological dysfunction, but Boorse and Wakefield use different accounts of function (Garson and Piccinini 2014). While Boorse characterizes the function of a trait in terms of its species-typical contribution to survival and reproduction, Wakefield's account of function is etiological and characterizes function in terms of the evolutionary history of a trait.

With respect to the value component, a dysfunction can only be classified as a disorder if it causes significant harm (Wakefield 2010, 284). Wakefield further argues that whether there is harm is determined by the standards of the prevailing societal and cultural context rather than by standards of the individual experiencing the condition. As cultures can embody different sets of values, the same trait with exactly the same effects can be a disorder in one culture but not in another. Wakefield maintains that in a literate society "a person who does not value reading still has a dyslexic disorder if incapable of learning to read due to a brain dysfunction" (Wakefield 2005, 98; see also De Block and Sholl 2021). In contrast, as we saw, other authors like Cooper (2002, 2005) maintain that individual differences in values matter for whether a condition is a disease: depending in part on what they value, a condition can be a bad thing and hence a disease for one person but not for another.

By combining a factual and a value component, hybridism captures the intuitions behind both naturalism and normativism and it addresses some of the challenges that plague these accounts. (We take intuitions to be tacit or explicit judgments or dispositions to judge that are not the result of one's theory about the topic of the intuitions.) For example, normativism is challenged by the compelling intuition that societies can erroneously classify certain conditions as diseases, such as masturbation, hysteria, and drapetomania in the nineteenth century (e.g., Ereshefsky 2009). The harmful dysfunction analysis counters this problem: although these conditions were disvalued, their classification as diseases was fundamentally mistaken because they did not involve any actual biological or psychological dysfunction. On the other hand, hybridism also inherits issues faced by normativism and naturalism. For instance, the harmful dysfunction analysis deems dysfunction necessary for a condition to be a disease, and as a result would fail to classify, implausibly, female anorgasmia as a disease if orgasms have no functional role in women (see Lloyd 2006 for a defense of this claim).

1.2 The Relational Issue

Most philosophers of medicine, including Boorse, Wakefield, and Cooper, subscribe to negativism about health. For negativists, health is just the absence of disease, which eliminates the need for separate analyses of health and disease. Negativism about health stands in contrast to positivism, which holds that health involves the presence of some positive states or capabilities (e.g., Nordenfelt 1995, 2017; Venkatapuram 2013; Wren-Lewis and Alexandrova 2021). Negativism is a common assumption in many accounts of health and disease and for many, it also appears intuitive: if a person has a disease, they are not healthy, and conversely, if a person is healthy, they do not have a disease. However, health might not solely be the absence or presence of disease. In particular, public health and rehabilitation medicine clearly deploy a "positive" concept of health, that is, a concept of health aligned with positivism (e.g., Nordenfelt 1998; Schramme 2017): if rehabilitative efforts aimed at improving function after the disease has been cured are considered *healthcare*, then health involves more than just not having a disease. Finally, people might seem to be healthy while having certain disabilities and effectively managed diseases (e.g., Venkatapuram 2013; Nordenfelt 2017; CDC 2020). Some authors also comprehend mental health and mental disorder not as opposite ends of one scale, but as two separate dimensions (e.g., Westerhof and Keyes 2010). On this view, the horizontal axis ranges from having no mental disorder symptoms to having a mental disorder, while the vertical axis ranges from optimal mental health ("flourishing") to poor mental health ("languishing").

1.3 Dysfunction

The notion of dysfunction plays an important role in the literature on health and disease, particularly for naturalists and hybridists, but dysfunctions and their relation to diseases are understood differently in the literature (e.g., Schwartz 2007a; Griffiths and Matthewson 2018; Garson 2019; Christie et al. 2023). Naturalists and hybridists agree that a condition counts as a disease only if it involves a dysfunction, and they also agree that the correct account of dysfunction is value-neutral, but, as we saw earlier, they disagree about whether functions are to be understood statistically (e.g., Boorse) or etiologically (e.g., Wakefield). Some normativists such as Cooper (2002, 2016) agree with naturalists that the correct account of dysfunction is not value-laden, but insist that whether a condition counts as a dysfunction is neither necessary nor sufficient for whether it is a disease (see also Kingma 2014; Muckler and Taylor 2020), a view we will call *narrow normativism*. Other normativists, embracing *wide normativism*, could agree with naturalists and hybridists that diseases require a dysfunction, while holding that the correct account of dysfunction is in fact value-laden. For example, Fulford argues that "dysfunction (…) has an essential evaluative (as well as a descriptive) element in its meaning" (Fulford 1999, 419; see also Fulford and Thornton 2007).

1.4 The Impasse and Two Problems in the Literature

The debate concerning health and disease features many intense and detailed exchanges and rebuttals that are far too intricate to capture in this brief summary. But many philosophers now argue that the philosophical debate has hit a standstill (Schwartz 2007a, 2007b, 2017; Lemoine 2013; Sholl 2015; Lemoine and Giroux 2016; Fuller 2018). Naturalist, normativist, and hybrid approaches may have succeeded in accommodating some set of intuitions regarding health and disease, but none of them provided a unified account capturing all relevant intuitions (Schwartz 2014; Gagné-Julien 2024). Numerous theorists have, more or less explicitly, pointed to various issues that have contributed to this deadlock. Some highlight methodological problems with conceptual analysis, while others point to the inherently irregular nature of the concepts of health and disease. In the following sections, we outline these issues and later demonstrate how the XPhiMed approach helps advance the debate.

Troubles with Conceptual Analysis

Some maintain that the stalled progress is partially due to the inherent limitations of the method that philosophers have deployed. Although the outlined approaches arrive at different conclusions about health and disease, they generally share a common methodology, as we noted earlier: they employ some form of conceptual analysis, a method that seeks to provide a descriptive (in contrast to prescriptive) definition of the meaning of a term or the content of a concept by examining its extension. As Lemoine (2013) explains, conceptual analysis typically begins by extensional stipulation, selecting uncontroversial cases from the extension of the terms or concepts. For example, when analyzing the meaning of "disease," the starting point would include instances such as tuberculosis or cancer, which undoubtedly qualify as diseases, and contrast these with conditions such as pregnancy or having red hair, which clearly do not fall under the concept of disease. Philosophers then attempt to establish a definition comprising a set of separately necessary and jointly sufficient criteria for a condition to count as a disease.

To offer an account of health or disease, philosophers thus use the "method of cases" to elicit intuitions or judgments: they describe, more or less extensively, actual or hypothetical conditions that people judge to be or not to be diseases or healthy. To the extent that judgments are guided by the content of the concept under investigation and not by other (e.g., pragmatic) factors, philosophers can explore cases along with the judgments they elicit, and infer the content of the concept (Goldman 2007). To challenge a competing account, philosophers present various hypothetical and real-world cases that fit the concept according to common usage but do not meet the account, cases that meet the account but are not typically included under the concept, and cases that the account cannot classify.

General problems with conceptual analysis and the method of cases have been extensively discussed in metaphilosophy (Machery 2017).

Here we focus on a more specific problem for the conceptual analysis of the concepts of health and disease. While philosophers agree that competing conceptual analyses should be constrained by uncontroversial cases (Barnes 2023, 15), most contemporary accounts tend to handle all the uncontroversial cases just fine. In such situations, conceptual analysis struggles to determine which of these competing accounts is the best, which has led some philosophers to argue that another method is needed (Lemoine 2013, 323–324).

Troubles with Irregular Concepts

Some have argued that the stalled progress in debates about the concepts of health and disease is partially due to their complex and perhaps irregular nature. Early on, Boorse (1975, 1997, 2011) noted that the existence of several "disease-plus" concepts – such as the concept of illness – complicates the analysis of health and disease. He suggests that an illness is a disease that is (a) undesirable for the person who has it, (b) warrants the person special treatment, and (c) is an excusing condition for ordinarily criticizable behavior. Others have, in various ways, maintained that there may be several concepts of health and disease that people deploy. For instance, Campbell, Scadding, and Roberts (1979) claim on the basis of a simple association task that there are multiple concepts of disease among lay people and medical practitioners. In line with this claim, some suggest that the concepts of health and disease serve a variety of purposes that may require more than one concept to fulfill (De Vreese 2017; van der Linden and Schermer 2024b). In more detail, Simon (2007) argues that "disease" does not express a single concept, but rather a family of polysemous concepts. So while the existing accounts of health appear to offer competing analyses of a single, general concept of disease, they could actually provide analyses of closely related, but distinct concepts.

Simon (2007, 361–362) offers a list of five conditions that "disease" can refer to depending on the context: (1) the suitable topics of medical scientific inquiry, (2) the physiological or psychological states that create a societal responsibility to care for those that have them, (3) the conditions that justify granting individuals the status of being sick and perhaps being relieved from certain duties, (4) the conditions whose diagnosis and treatment fall within the limits of medical practice, and (5) the conditions whose presence implies that doctors ought to act to treat them. So perhaps naturalists target (1) or (4), normativists (2), (3), or perhaps (5), and hybridists perhaps a combination of some of them. To offer a unifying analysis of disease, one of the meanings of "disease" would have to be fundamental, and the others would have to depend on it.

Similarly, Barnes (2023) stresses that the concept of health has multiple roles of varying significance (including biological, normative, political, and phenomenological significance) that a successful account of health is expected to cover. Barnes (2023, 2–6) points out the unresolvable tensions between these roles and concludes that, as a result, it is not possible to provide a single, coherent, extensionally adequate account of health. For instance, when one gives due consideration to the biological significance of health, one is likely to inadvertently downplay its normative and phenomenological significance, and vice versa (Barnes 2023, 247): one is likely to overlook that a decreased health is not just a decline in objective functional status, but also a morally significant harm, while also neglecting the phenomenological dimensions of health, which are experienced uniquely by each individual (Barnes 2023, 203).

The difficulty in giving due to all the dimensions of health leads Barnes to embrace a skeptical conclusion and proposes abandoning the fruitless search for a unified account: there is no clear, coherent thing that it is to be healthy. Instead, when we talk about health, we are loosely tracking a range of features, and while various philosophical attempts might give us insights into these features, they fail to give us a unified account. Barnes does not call for eliminating the concept of health, but she also maintains that separating out the different features for different purposes is not productive, because that would mean losing the interconnectedness and interdependence inherent to health.

1.5 Ways Forward

There are at least three different ways to advance the debates about health and disease. First, according to the *eliminativist approach*, given the hopelessly muddled discourse surrounding health and disease, we should abandon the respective concepts altogether (e.g., Hesslow 1993). Second, according to the *engineering approach*, we should abandon a descriptive conceptual analysis and aim instead to offer an explication or a revisionary account (e.g., Kukla 2022). This approach is informed by recent work on conceptual engineering, according to which the goal is not to describe the content of concepts, but to actively revise them to enhance precision or further social justice objectives (Machery 2017; Cappelen 2018). Third, according to the *experimental approach*, we should enhance traditional conceptual analysis by incorporating empirical methods from fields like experimental philosophy (e.g., Walker and Rogers 2018; De Block and Hens 2021; Faucher 2021; Faucher and Béghin 2023; Hens and De Block 2023). We should thus use the tools of experimental philosophy to investigate the concepts of health and disease, in line with the idea of "naturalized conceptual analysis" (Machery 2017). Wakefield himself clearly sees a role for empirical approaches, as he notes that conceptual analysis is "a form of psychological theorizing about shared cognitive structures underlying shared classificatory judgments. (…) Empirical studies thus have an important role as an adjunct to conceptual analysis if designed, executed, and interpreted with care" (Wakefield 2021, 73).

In this Element, we embrace the experimental approach (XPhiMed), highlighting its potential to enrich the debates about the concepts of health and disease. Of course, one could empirically discover that people are hopelessly confused about health and disease and so uncover evidence that could be used to motivate the eliminativist approach. However, the concepts of health and disease are not only integral to everyday language and medical practice, but are also pivotal in public health communication and ethical discussions regarding medical duties and rights. Further, as we will show in this Element, we think that empirical evidence to date shows people are not hopelessly confused at all. As such we should reject the eliminativist approach. There are also reasons to think that the engineering approach would significantly benefit from XPhiMed. In what follows, we describe XPhiMed as an experimentally driven, descriptive, and ameliorative endeavor, suggesting it is well suited to address methodological limitations and handle complex and perhaps irregular concepts such as HEALTH and DISEASE.

1.6 Experimental Philosophy of Medicine (XPhiMed)

Experimental philosophy employs empirical methods, typically associated with psychology, cognitive science, and sociology, to inform philosophical inquiries (e.g., Knobe 2003; Machery et al. 2004; Knobe et al. 2012). It deploys surveys, experiments, and other data collection techniques to gather information about people's judgments on topics of philosophical interest (e.g., Sytsma and Livengood 2015; Kornmesser et al. 2024). Many studies examine patterns of judgments to systematically varied scenarios ("vignettes") to gather evidence about the content of concepts and the cognitive processes that use them. Experimental philosophy has had significant impact across various philosophical domains, yet its application within the philosophy of medicine remains curiously limited. This oversight is especially notable considering the substantial experimental work on scientific concepts such as the concepts of gene, innateness, and representation (Stotz and Griffiths 2004; Griffiths et al. 2009; Machery 2016; Machery et al. 2019; Favela and Machery 2023).

XPhiMed can obviously assist in describing the content of the concepts of health and disease, directly addressing some of the methodological limitations highlighted in the previous sections. Experimental (e.g., Stich and Machery 2023) and traditional (e.g., Katz and Fodor 1962) philosophers have often criticized the method of cases for relying on the judgments of philosophers, which may not accurately reflect the judgments of the general population whose conceptual usage philosophers purportedly track. Instead, the empirical methods of experimental philosophy allow gathering more representative judgments from diverse populations, ensuring that philosophical analyses are better grounded in the actual content of the target concepts. If some project in the philosophy of medicine involves understanding the concepts of health and disease, we recommend philosophers embrace the kind of experimental methodology illustrated by the rest of this Element, perhaps in conjunction with other empirical methods such as text-analytic techniques (e.g., Buts et al. 2021). While this is not our focus here, the claim about the usefulness of this methodology is not limited to the concepts of health and disease, but extends to a broader range of health-related concepts.

For instance, as noted earlier, conceptual analysis typically begins by selecting allegedly uncontroversial cases from the extension of the concepts. XPhiMed can empirically test this assumption, putting philosophical theorizing on a more empirically solid footing. Besides examining this kind of assumption, XPhiMed can provide evidence bearing on specific accounts of health and disease, such as Barnes's proposal that the concept of health is about something akin to the well-being of organisms or Simon's claim about the polysemy of "disease."

Further, experimental methods can be used to determine which properties influence the application of the concepts of health, disease, and dysfunction. Assuming that these concepts do not have necessary and sufficient conditions, but rather are composed of a cluster of represented properties, some of them are more central to or influential in how the concept is applied. Experimental philosophy can be employed to empirically investigate which properties are most crucial for concept application and examine also whether these properties vary across contexts or differ across demographic groups.

Moreover, as Chalmers (2020) has argued, philosophically interesting terms might often express several concepts, each serving a distinct role.

One philosophical task is to articulate these roles clearly and to determine which concepts most effectively fulfill them. Extending an idea inspired by Stotz and Griffiths's experimental work and following the lead of Barnes, we may conceptualize this task as exploring the "conceptual ecology" of health and disease concepts. Such an investigation into conceptual ecology would examine how different concepts of health and disease coexist and adapt to meet varying theoretical and practical demands across diverse contexts. XPhiMed can also lay the groundwork for an ameliorative project. An investigation revealing that the concepts of health and disease are applied in inconsistent and unproductive ways could legitimize conceptual revision (or elimination). Conceptual revision would aim at ensuring that the concepts of health and disease fulfill their intended functions more effectively and distinctly than the existing concepts. Besides enhancing conceptual clarity, this revision could also improve the practical utility of these concepts, contributing to more targeted and effective applications in medicine, public health, or policymaking. If the concept (or perhaps concepts) of health serves multiple and sometimes conflicting roles, with the specific role determined by the context in which it is used, employing more precise concepts tailored to the particular aspects of health being discussed in each context could improve communication and decision-making. For example, if using a negativist conception of health (as mere absence of disease) in public health policies or in clinical practices is out of step with the public's understanding of health, which could include psychological resilience and social well-being, then there is a clear reason for revision.

The aim of XPhiMed as a descriptive and ameliorative endeavor is not necessarily to provide a single, concise account of health and disease, which may not be feasible given the complexity and variability of these concepts. XPhiMed can instead map out the variation in how these concepts are understood, explore the causes and consequences of this variation, and propose ameliorative adjustments.

1.7 Objections to XPhiMed

Proponents of both descriptive projects and ameliorative approaches may regard XPhiMed with skepticism, questioning whether understanding people's concepts of health and disease through empirical methods should carry significant implications for philosophical debates. After all, they might argue, such discussions are typically reserved for professional philosophers and should not rely heavily on commonsense understanding; at most, a theory of health and disease should concern itself only with medical professionals' concepts, as restricted accounts propose. However, this concern is unwarranted for several reasons.

First, appeals to lay judgments regarding health and disease have played a key role in the relevant debates (Murphy 2021), and it is of course important for philosophers to probe empirically whether the assumptions they make about common sense judgments are correct. Furthermore, as discussed in relation to unrestricted accounts, many theorists take themselves to be describing both professional and lay concepts of disease and health. For instance, from the hybridist camp, Wakefield and Conrad (2020, 363) explicitly state that harmful dysfunction analysis is an analysis that can "explain professional medical and lay shared judgments of disorder and nondisorder in terms of background beliefs about dysfunction and values." Wakefield himself has used empirical methods to investigate aspects of the harmful dysfunction analysis (Wakefield et al. 2006). Some normativists also argue that conceptual analysis should align with laypeople's intuitions. For example, Cooper (2020, 144) maintains that "in so far as philosophers seeking to develop accounts of disorder engage in descriptive conceptual analysis, accounts must broadly fit with intuitions about the disorder status of particular conditions."

What's more, the concepts of health and disease do not primarily live in the thoughts of philosophers of medicine; they do not even primarily live in those of medical professionals. Rather, they circulate between lay people and medical professionals, and they play an important role in the communication between them. While this circulation does not entail that medical professionals and lay people have identical concepts, it suggests that their concepts are probably not too different. Furthermore, even if medical professionals' concepts differ from those of lay people in important respects (perhaps in different respects in different areas of medicine), understanding lay concepts might still be relevant from a philosophical point of view, perhaps to better understand the relations between lay and scientific concepts, or perhaps to remedy the shortcomings of medical communication among nonprofessionals, perhaps to ensure that medical professionals' concepts have not drifted too far apart from what health and diseases are for lay people. It is also worth noting that an experimental method could be applied to medical professionals' concepts themselves: the experimental method is not bound to studying lay concepts. Finally, and more radically, one could hold that the true home of the concepts of health and disease is in lay cognition, in how human beings experience their own condition in relation to their environment, and that any divergence of a technical concept from this true home is a betrayal.

Second, those pursuing an ameliorative rather than descriptive approach might also question the relevance of empirically understanding people's concepts of health and disease. Proponents of conceptual engineering do not seek to describe the meaning or usage of concepts, but to actively reform them, providing new definitions to enhance their utility in specific contexts (e.g., Burgess and Plunkett 2013a, 2013b; Cappelen 2018). As we saw, within the health and disease debate, some advocate engineering as an alternative (e.g., Carel 2007, 2008; Schwartz 2014; Kukla 2022). So if conceptual analysis has exposed the problematic nature of the concepts of health and disease, why continue to invest effort in understanding their content instead of developing new concepts that more effectively serve their functions?

However, whether engineering projects are justified hinges on whether the diagnosis about existing concepts is descriptively accurate (e.g., Machery 2017; Cooper 2020). Additionally, grounding conceptual engineering in experimental philosophy might help respect limitations that commonsense use sets on engineering projects (Machery 2017; Schupbach 2017). As Murphy (2021) puts it, "everyday language puts constraints on a concept of health that need to be respected, and that if we move too far from ordinary usage we have stopped talking about health and started talking about something else." In a similar fashion, Matthewson and Griffiths (2017, 450) argue that common analyses of health and disease are insufficient if they fail to include conditions generally recognized as diseases. Of course, this does not mean that accounts of health and disease that deviate from commonsense use are not perfectly good accounts of something. However, they might not be accounts of health and disease, at least in the sense that frames most ordinary thought. Finally, experimental work is needed to address "implementation issues" in conceptual engineering, namely how to actually modify people's concepts in light of recommended revisions (Machery 2025).

1.8 XPhiMed in Light of Sociological, Anthropological, and Psychological Research

While experimental philosophy has not yet systematically tackled the concepts of health and disease, there is substantial existing research across disciplines such as anthropology, sociology, and psychology. Most studies target illness-specific beliefs within specific at-risk or afflicted populations, and comparatively few explore the general public's concepts of health (Hughner and Kleine 2004; for mental disorders, see Tse and Haslam 2023; for a review, see Faucher and Béghin 2023). Although a comprehensive review of this interdisciplinary literature is beyond our scope, we will outline some key aspects of this research and show how the methods of experimental philosophy can offer complementary insights (see also Faucher and Béghin 2023; Machery 2023, Section 1). It is important to note that our discussion simplifies a complex field that encompasses diverse approaches.

The relevant studies in health anthropology, sociology, and psychology predominantly employ qualitative methods, capturing the richness of individual perspectives through detailed, open-ended interviews and written surveys. This is typically combined with quantitative analysis to detect associations between specific concepts of health and other factors such as health status, health behaviors, and socioeconomic status. Classic studies investigated health concepts in France (Herzlich 1973; d'Houtaud and Field 1984), Scotland (Williams 1983), the United States (Millstein and Irwin 1987), and Great Britain (Blaxter 1990). A common feature across such studies involves posing open-ended questions such as "According to you (the layperson), what is health?", "Describe a healthy person you know?", or "What is it like when you are healthy?". This qualitative approach yields rich descriptions and complex participant accounts, revealing that concepts of health are deeply entangled in individuals' life histories and are applied inconsistently (for discussion, see Blaxter 2010).

Researchers typically code participants' responses to identify recurring "themes" from the data obtained through qualitative methods. While many of these themes are similar and overlap across different studies, there are instances where the findings significantly differ. For example, early studies showed that lay concepts exhibit multiple dimensions (e.g., health as a reserve or capacity, as the absence of illness, or as equilibrium and balance) (Herzlich 1973; Williams 1983). Millstein and Erwin (1987) distinguish between the following themes: preventive-maintenance behavior (e.g., eating a good diet), affective states (e.g., having a good attitude), functional capacity (e.g., easy to run a mile), somatic feeling states (e.g., feeling good), and no diseases (e.g., not getting the flu). The authors find that somatic feeling states, preventive-maintenance behaviors, and functional status are the most often recurring themes (Millstein and Erwin 1987, 518). Fugelli and Ingstad (2001) identify six themes: well-being, function, nature, a sense of humor, coping, and energy. Blaxter (1990; 2010) delineates nine distinct themes: living a healthy lifestyle, physical fitness, the absence of disease, having a reserve, being able to do things, psychosocial well-being, vitality, good social relationships, and something one can have in spite of having disease.

In their comprehensive review of the literature, Hughner and Kleine (2004) find eighteen different themes across studies about the lay concept of health. Highlighting the most common ones, Hughner and Kleine (2004) and Bishop and Yardley (2010) identify three to five major themes. These included viewing health as the absence of illness, as the ability to perform daily activities, and as the experience of vitality and balance. More recently, Downey and Chang (2013) employed open-ended questioning and progressively refined qualitative responses to identify four dominant themes: adequate rest, social-emotional health, absence of stress and anxiety, and positive health practices.

Overall, the qualitative methods employed in these studies provide rich insights into lay concepts, highlighting the complexity and significance of health for these populations. However, researchers such as Hughner and Kleine (2004) have suggested that to obtain a fuller understanding, it would be beneficial to integrate these qualitative insights with quantitative methods.

Furthermore, these studies are not equipped to explore how these themes can come apart and conflict in different contexts. Tellingly, researchers sometimes interpret their results as indicating that lay people have several distinct concepts of health (e.g., one referring to the absence of illness and one referring to the functional capacity to fulfill social role obligations, see Calnan 1987), while others posit several, distinct aspects of a single, multidimensional concept. This ambiguity could be addressed by experimental approaches that can systematically manipulate and isolate these themes to better understand their relationships and significance for how people understand health. Such experimental designs could manipulate one particular theme while keeping others constant to see how this manipulation affects people's judgments, clarifying how much this theme matters to the concept of health.

The second limitation concerns asking participants to define health directly. This task can be challenging because individuals might not have explicit access to the full content of the concepts under investigation, which are typically deployed tacitly in everyday contexts. Participants might thus struggle to articulate these concepts comprehensively, leading to potential mismatches between their everyday usage and the responses gathered through direct questioning. To overcome this, experimental methods could be instrumental in designing studies that probe implicit understandings of health and disease.

1.9 XPhiMed and the Contrastive Vignette Method

Vignette experiments use brief, systematically varied scenarios to investigate participants' judgments in response to these scenarios. Vignettes offer several advantages over traditional survey questions, enhancing a study's internal and construct validity as well as its reliability (Steiner et al. 2016). They provide more concrete scenarios than abstract survey questions, allow for the analysis of multiple factors and their interactions simultaneously, and can reduce socially desirable or politically correct responses on sensitive topics.

Contrastive experimental vignettes approaches favored in experimental philosophy use a sequence of vignettes that are identical except for one or several elements varied to assess how this change influences participants' responses. They typically employ a between-subjects design, meaning that each participant is only exposed to one version of the vignette. This experimental design allows for the exploration of how specific factors influence judgments in ways that might be challenging or unethical to test in real-life situations.

For illustration of how such studies could be structured, let us consider the theme "health as the absence of disease," which has been highlighted in both the studies reviewed earlier and the philosophical debates on health and disease. XPhiMed researchers could create a series of vignettes, each depicting an individual with varying health profiles. Specifically, each vignette would feature a person who is free from any disease but exhibits different levels of other health-related themes such as "vitality and balance" or "capability to perform daily activities." Participants in the study would be randomly assigned to different vignettes and instructed to assess the health status of the depicted individual. This method allows determining whether the absence of disease, by itself, is sufficient for participants to consider someone as healthy, thereby isolating and highlighting its perceived importance in the lay conception of health. This setup can provide valuable insights into how this theme interacts with other health dimensions and influences overall health judgments.

This brief example illustrates how XPhiMed could clarify whether certain themes like "health as the absence of disease" are fundamental to the concept of health or if they are more peripheral. This approach avoids the assumption that people can explicitly articulate their concepts of health and disease. Instead, XPhiMed proposes using experimental methods to study people's judgments, suggesting that these judgments provide defeasible evidence for the content of concepts such as HEALTH and DISEASE, even if their content is implicit. Moreover, by analyzing responses across various scenarios, XPhiMed can uncover the factors that influence decisions to classify conditions as healthy or as diseases and explore how these judgments vary across demographic groups.

2 Health

People often consult with healthcare providers not only because of symptoms of illness but also to proactively monitor their health status. Indeed, the yearly medical visit to the general practitioner that is recommended in the USA is often called a "health checkup" (and "bilan de santé" in France). Additionally, this focus on health is evident in the proliferation of "health and wellness" sections in bookstores, which offer an array of popular literature on healthy lifestyles, living, and eating. Undeniably, throughout relatively affluent Western countries, there is a marked preoccupation with all things health related.

A search on Google's Ngram viewer (10/02/2024) suggests that the nine most common nouns qualified by "healthy" in English are "controls," "individuals," "diet," "life," "subjects," "people," "volunteers," "children," and "growth" (see also Reuter, Latham, and Varga 2025). It appears that in contemporary English "healthy" is most commonly used to qualify either people (e.g., control participants in a randomized controlled trial) or conditions related to the health of individuals: a healthy diet is one that either contributes to or is constitutive of the health of people following this diet. Figure 1 plots the frequency of some of these expressions together with "healthy mind" and "healthy liver" ("healthy lungs" gives similar results).[1]

Figure 1 suggests that "healthy" is nowadays less frequently used to qualify body parts ("liver" is not unusual in this respect), including internal organs, than to qualify persons or their habits and activities. It also provides evidence for a surge of interest in the activities and habits associated

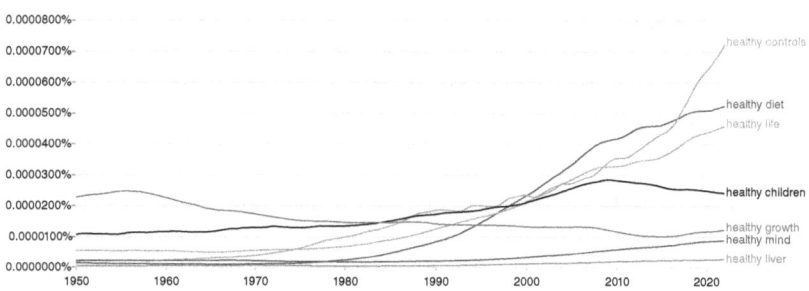

Figure 1 Ngram for Six Expressions Involving "Healthy" from 1950 to 2022 (from Google Books Ngram Viewer, http://books.google.com/ngrams)

---

[1] Ngram plots the proportion of words of a given length among words of that length in the books scanned by Google.

with a "healthy lifestyle" after 1980, such as a healthy diet (the greater frequency of "healthy controls" is itself plausibly due to the increasing significance of the biomedical sciences in Western science).

So, what do people mean by "health" such that it can be applied to persons and to activities and habits? As we explained in Section 1, some philosophers and some medical practitioners have identified health with the absence of diseases (a position we called "negativism"), while others reject this negative concept of health, either defining it as some form of well-being or identifying it with the possession of some capacities (e.g., resilience or the capacities needed to reach some goals).

2.1 Is Health Merely the Absence of Diseases?

To examine whether lay people conceive of health as just the absence of diseases, Varga and Latham (2024a) conducted a study with English-speaking participants from the USA, who were recruited online. The participants were presented with a vignette describing either someone who has no symptoms, but is diagnosed with a disease (celiac disease) or someone who does not have any symptoms, but has vitals close to those indicating some pathology. If people embrace a negative concept of health, they should be less likely to find the first person to be healthy than the second. The first vignette read as follows:

> **Mila**
> Mila lives an active lifestyle and at her yearly check-up tells her physician that she is feeling great. The physician informs Mila that while all her test results are normal (blood pressure, cholesterol, triglycerides, body mass index, and so on), she has tested positive for celiac disease. People with celiac disease have an immune response to eating gluten which can damage the intestinal lining preventing the absorption of some nutrients, and can cause diarrhea, fatigue, weight loss, and anemia. Mila would never have known that she had celiac disease had the physician not performed the test. That's because Mila never eats gluten and lives in a gluten-free community.

By contrast, the second vignette read as follows:

> **Luca**
> Luca lives a sedentary lifestyle and at her yearly check-up tells her physician that she is feeling ok. The physician informs Luca both that she is disease free and that all her test results are normal. However, the physician also tells Luca that while her blood pressure, cholesterol, triglycerides, body mass index, and so on, are all within the normal range, they are *all* very close to being classed as abnormal.

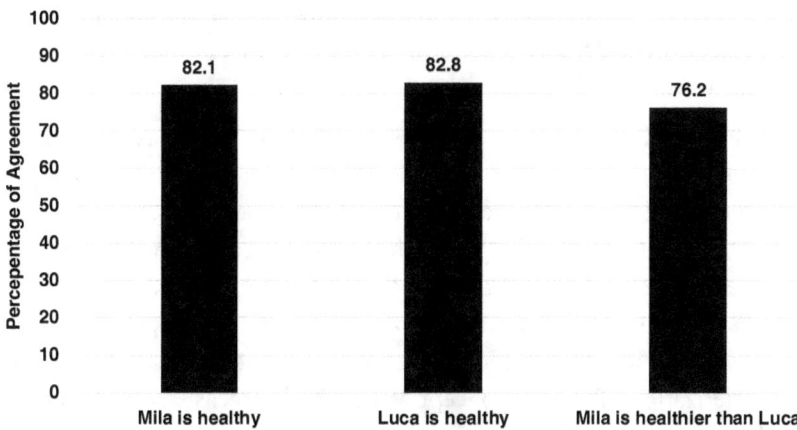

Figure 2 Proportion of Participants Answering "Yes," "Yes," and "Mila" in Study 1 of Varga and Latham (2024a)

Participants were asked three questions: whether Mila/Luca is healthy (yes/no answer), whether they have a disease (yes/no answer), and who they thought is healthier, Mila or Luca. Before looking at how participants answered, try answering these three questions yourself. To see participants' answers, look at Figure 2.

Most people, then, believe that one can have a disease such as celiac disease and be healthy, at least provided that the disease is asymptomatic and has a "conditional" nature (i.e., the symptoms are only present when people are exposed to some external circumstances).

In the vignette developed by Varga and Latham, Mila is not at risk of having a symptomatic condition, while Luca is. One might wonder whether the judgment that Mila is healthier than Luca is due to this difference: would the results be the same if Mila was at risk of experiencing the symptoms of celiac disease? To examine this question, Varga and Latham developed a second pair of vignettes.

Mila
Mila lives an active lifestyle and at her yearly check-up tells her physician that while she has generally felt good, recently she has been experiencing both diarrhea and feeling fatigued. The physician informs Mila that while all her test results are normal (blood pressure, cholesterol, triglycerides, body mass index, and so on), she has tested positive for celiac disease. People with celiac disease have an immune response to eating gluten which can damage to the intestinal lining preventing the absorption of some nutrients, and can cause diarrhea, fatigue, weight loss, and anemia. The physician informs Mila that she can successfully manage her condition by avoiding gluten in her diet. Mila tells her physician that this should not be

a problem for her. Gluten-free food products are readily available in her community, and they do not cost any more than ordinary gluten-inclusive products. She also prefers the taste of gluten-free products.

In addition to being at risk of developing symptoms, Mila has also already experienced the symptoms characteristic of her condition in the past. The Luca vignette was not changed. Figure 3 reports the results.

The results are largely similar to those observed in Study 1, suggesting that being healthy is thought to be consistent with having an asymptomatic disease even when one is at risk of experiencing its symptoms.

These results are compelling evidence that negativism is not a correct characterization of the lay concept of health for at least Americans since for lay people being healthy is consistent with having a disease (see also Bushnell et al. 2000; De Jong et al. 2020). This finding is consistent with the frequent use of the word "healthy" to qualify activities and habits that are not just aimed at eliminating diseases or preventing their occurrence.

Nonetheless, this study is limited in several respects. First, it is not clear whether some version of positivism characterizes the lay concept of health for all or most human populations: could there be some cultural, historical, socioeconomic, or other demographic variation? Are some factors, such as personality, gender, social class, profession, and past medical history (see Simon et al. 2005; Huber et al. 2016), more likely to incline people to have a negative understanding of health? We begin addressing these questions in Section 2.3. Second, the scope of positivism is unclear: is the failure of negativism limited to celiac disease (which might appear to some as an allergy rather than a prototypical disease),

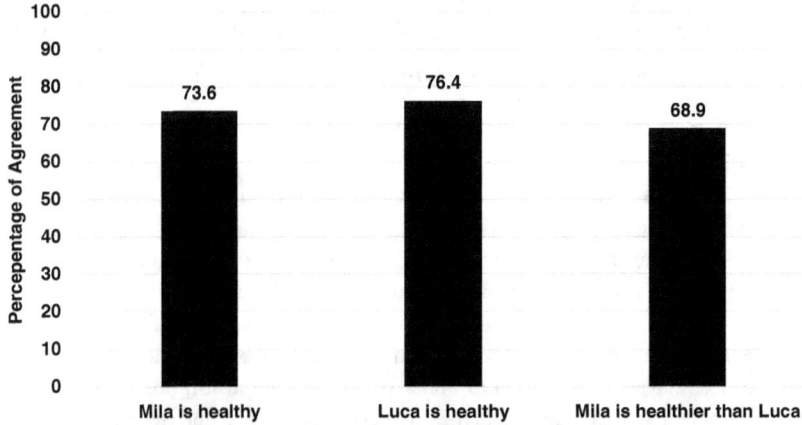

Figure 3 Proportion of Participants Answering "Yes," "Yes," and "Mila" in Study 2 of Varga and Latham (2024a)

to chronic diseases such as type 1 diabetes, to asymptomatic diseases, or, perhaps, to diseases whose symptomatic manifestation depends on external conditions? Would people make similar judgments if a disease's symptoms were repressed by drugs or if it were not a chronic disease? Study 2 of Varga and Latham (2024a) also shows that being at risk of experiencing the symptoms of a disease is consistent with being healthy, although it remains unclear whether this is true for all forms of risk and all degrees of risk: would Mila be judged healthy if she were extremely likely to experience the symptoms of celiac disease every other day? Exploring this scenario invites further investigation into how lay judgments vary across different types of risk, including genetic, environmental, and behavioral factors. Additional research is needed to answer these questions, but Section 2.4 takes a stab at them.

Third, while these results suggest that negativism is wrong[2] – in the sense that it is not the case that for most people, health reduces to the absence of disease – they reveal little about the concept of health entertained by lay people. Could one experience some symptoms of a disease and still be healthy or, rather, does health require the complete absence of a symptom? In the latter case, what more is required to be healthy? Is it complete well-being as proposed by the World Health Organization, or some capacities related to well-being, or something else entirely different? Section 2.3 begins examining these questions.

Finally, the results reported so far are about the *lay* concept of health. Would medical practitioners make similar judgments to those made by lay people? Fortunately, Varga and Latham have already taken steps to examine that question.

2.2 Positivism and Negativism among Medical Practitioners

As we noted in Section 1, philosophers disagree about whether their theories about health are meant to be about health as understood by medical practitioners, or perhaps a subset of them, as Boorse proposes, or about health as understood by both lay people and medical practitioners, as Wakefield proposes. It is certainly possible that the concept of health differs between lay people and some or all medical practitioners. To examine the question, Varga and Latham (2024a) also conducted the two studies

---

[2] This finding is however consistent with the idea that lay people have multiple concepts of health – one that defines health negatively as the absence of disease and another that defines health positively (see the discussion on the possible plurality of concepts of health and disease in Section 1).

discussed in Section 2.1 with undergraduate medical students from Aarhus University in Denmark. Figures 4 and 5 report the results.

Medical students seem somewhat more sensitive to risk when making health judgments, but their responses are overall very similar to those of lay people. They too tend to endorse some version of positivism, although, as is the case with lay people, it is not clear which form of positivism they endorse. Future research should examine whether this pattern of judgments reflects the fact that students have not yet developed a fully mature technical understanding of health and whether more seasoned medical practitioners understand health differently. It is also possible that while

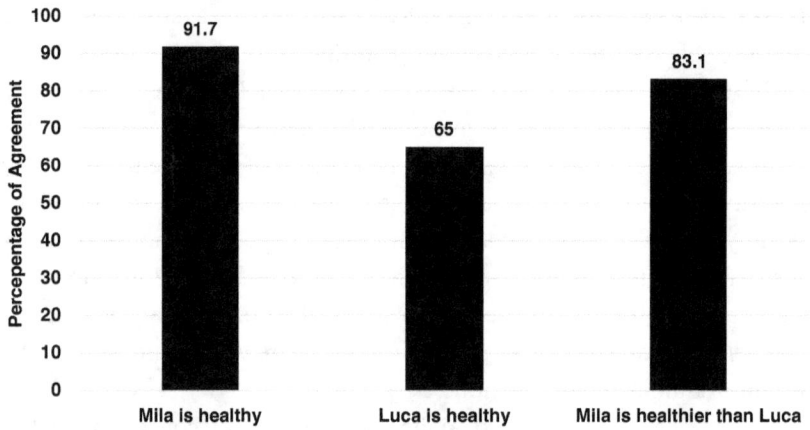

Figure 4 Proportion of Medical Student Participants Answering "Yes," "Yes," and "Mila" in Study 1 of Varga and Latham 2024a

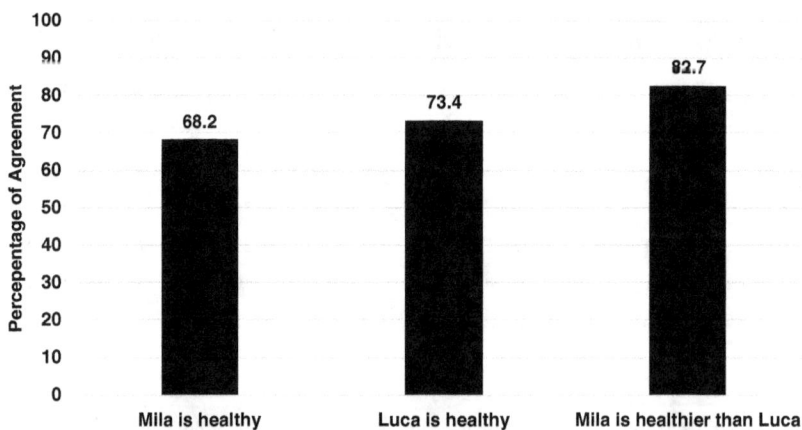

Figure 5 Proportion of Medical Student Participants Answering "Yes," "Yes," and "Mila" in Study 2 of Varga and Latham 2024a

many lay people and medical practitioners reject negativism, their positive understanding of health differs. Finally, it could be that different groups of medical practitioners understand health differently: perhaps researchers engaged in the most fundamental, less applied part of the biomedical sciences have a strictly negative concept of health. Or practitioners who have a less patient-facing activity (pathologists, etc.) might be more likely than those with a more patient-facing activity (e.g., general practitioners) to have a strictly negative concept of health.

2.3 Health and Lifestyle

The meaning of words changes over time, and "health" is plausibly not an exception, although few philosophers have paid attention to this point (see Cooper 2020, esp. 141–142, for a notable exception). Reuter, Latham, and Varga (2025) have argued that the contemporary concept of health has evolved since 1980 (with the growing influence of preventive medicine, as manifested by the dietary guidelines, the stress on exercise, and so on), and that it is now primarily applied to various aspects of lifestyle: physical activities, diet, and other habits.[3] Thus, examining both in corpora and by utilizing N-grams (as we did above in the introduction of this section following their lead) how often and in which context "healthy" is used, Reuter and colleagues highlight the "predominant association of the term 'healthy' with lifestyle-related matters such as eating, food, and diet since the 1980s" (but see Simon et al. 2005 who report that only 3% of Dutch participants mentioned practices and habits in semi-structured interviews).

To confirm the centrality of lifestyle in the contemporary concept of health, Reuter and colleagues used "a feature production task," a task often used in psychology to study prototypes (Machery 2009). Reuter and colleagues' version of this task consists simply in asking participants to "name three features that [they] believe are characteristic of being unhealthy," or "sick." Two findings emerge from this study. First, in line with Varga and Latham's findings, "unhealthy" and "sick" are not synonyms, contrary to what we would have expected if negativism were true. People list mostly symptoms of diseases when they generate features associated with "sick": "cough," "fever," or "temperature." By contrast, and this is the second finding, people tend to generate activities, habits, and characteristics related to lifestyle when asked to generate features associated with "unhealthy": "overweight,"

---

[3] We are not claiming that the 1980s were the first time a positive concept of health gained wide currency. For all we know, some positive concept or other might have already been common a century ago, to be replaced, perhaps, by a negative concept of health.

"smoking," or "lazy." We interpret these results as providing evidence about the differences between the prototypes associated with "sick" and "unhealthy." These two findings are confirmed in a recent vignette study by Reuter, Latham, and Varga (2025). Participants recruited online were presented with one of two vignettes. A first vignette described someone with no disease but a negatively valued lifestyle, while the second vignette described her as having a positive lifestyle.

> **Negative Lifestyle**
> During the last six months, Erica has not had any diseases like infections, inflammations or bodily malfunctions. During the last six months, Erica has also not experienced any symptoms like headaches, fever, or nausea. During the last six months, Erica has not exercised, slept little, was under a lot of stress, ate poorly, and smoked a lot.[4]
>
> **Positive Lifestyle**
> During the last six months, Erica has not had any diseases like infections, inflammations or bodily malfunctions. During the last six months, Erica has also not experienced any symptoms like headaches, fever, or nausea. During the last six months, Erica has exercised regularly, slept sufficiently, ate properly, and did not smoke.

Participants were then asked to assess whether Erica was healthy, unhealthy, and sick on a 7-point Likert scale measuring agreement from 1 (strongly disagree), through 4 (neutral), to 7 (strongly agree). Figure 6 reports the results.

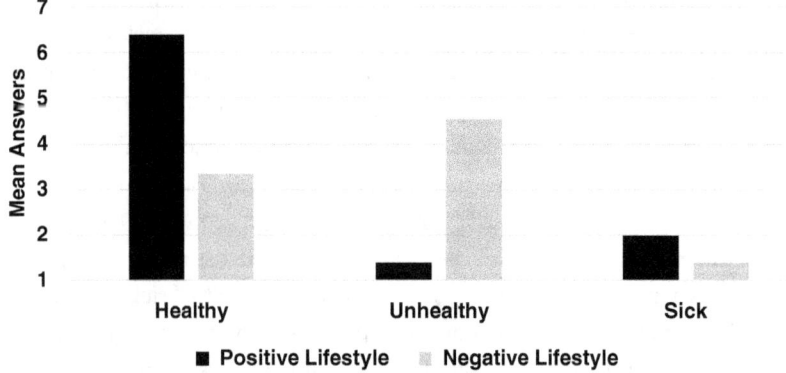

Figure 6 Results of Vignette Study 1 in Reuter et al. (2025)

---

[4] We note that medical professionals might not find this vignette plausible since smoking can increase inflammation throughout the body. We doubt however that lay people are aware of this fact.

Study 1 suggests "unhealthy" and "sick" are not synonymous. Perhaps, however, Study 1 results were found for one of the three following reasons: participants might have understood "unhealthy" as "psychologically unhealthy"; they might have assumed that Erica has in fact a disease despite having been symptom-free for the last six months; or they might have thought that her "unhealthy" lifestyle is putting her at risk of falling sick. A follow up study (Reuter, Latham, and Varga 2025, Study 2) replicated Study 1's result and provided evidence against these three interpretations. Asking people to evaluate Erica's "physical" health as opposed to just health or, adding to the vignette that Erica was either disease free or naturally immune to the negative consequences of her unhealthy lifestyle, had *no* influence on participants' "unhealthy" judgments.

Thus, "sick" and "unhealthy" appear not to be synonymous, providing further evidence against negativism. Furthermore, lifestyle matters for the application of the concepts expressed by "healthy" and "unhealthy," but not for the concept expressed by "sick." Reuter and colleagues' findings speak to the questions we raised above. First, we can now go beyond the mere claim that negativism does not correctly describe medical students' and lay people's contemporary concept of health. To be healthy is, in part, to have a particular lifestyle involving some habits and practices (e.g., exercising) in addition perhaps to be free of symptoms (even if one has a disease, as we saw in Section 2.1). Other habits and practices (e.g., smoking and overeating) are thought to render people unhealthy.

A deflationary, negativism-friendly explanation of this finding proposes that what unifies these practices is that they all reduce the risk of falling sick and contracting a disease – on this view, the concept of health would still represent health as more than just the absence of a disease, but would be dependent on this latter concept – but Reuter and colleagues' Study 2 provides some evidence against this explanation: even when there is no such risk (because the character is said to be naturally immune to the negative consequences of her unhealthy lifestyle), people still judge that overeating and not exercising make people unhealthy.

Alternative explanations propose that the concept of health is positive. Perhaps health is identical to well-being and the activities and habits mentioned in the positive lifestyle vignette quoted above ("exercised regularly, slept sufficiently, ate properly, and did not smoke") are either constitutive or indicative of well-being; instead, health might be identical to capabilities that allow people to achieve some goals and again the activities and habits mentioned in the positive lifestyle vignette are somehow related to these capabilities. The results do not speak about which of these alternative explanations is correct. We caution however the reader against expecting either lay people's or professional practitioners' concepts to make deep philosophical sense: the concept of health could just be a prototype, representing activities and characteristics typically associated with healthy people (more on this idea below); second and related to the first point, the concept of health could merely represent what happens to be salient in the surrounding culture.

It would be remiss of us to ignore the potential for injustice present in a positive prototype of health built around diet, control of calorie intake, and physical activities. First, we note that it is not entirely clear whether the activities and characteristics commonsensically associated with an unhealthy lifestyle are all actually harmful (see, e.g., Manne 2025). Second, whether people are able to pursue and enjoy elements of a healthy lifestyle depends in part on their environments and their socioeconomic status (it is much harder to have a balanced diet when you are poor and live in the middle of a food desert; see Beaulac et al. 2009); by contrast, one is led to think of activities and habits like diet and physical exercise as the kind of things people have control over (if only obese people had more willpower!) when one conceptualizes them as part of a lifestyle (lifestyles, one might be inclined to think, erroneously we submit, are the kind of things people choose; see van der Heijden et al. 2021 on healthy diet). Third, the particular focus on lifestyle characteristics such as diet and exercise might reflect the priorities of people with high socioeconomic status (Stronks et al. 2018; see also d'Houtaud and Field 1984, which we discuss below). For instance, Stronks and colleagues find that low socioeconomic status people associate health with access to healthcare, while high socioeconomic status people do not, possibly because having access to healthcare is so obvious that it is not noticeable to them.

Reuter and colleagues' study has allowed us to begin addressing some of the questions flagged earlier, but much remains uncertain. Our understanding of the concept of health remains limited: what kind of positivism is closer to the lay concept of health? It is also unclear how medical practitioners think about health and whether there is variation among different areas of medicine and biomedical research. Even when limiting our claim to lay people, it is not clear whether there is demographic variation in the endorsement of a positive concept of health. In this regard, Reuter and colleagues note that a quarter of their participants in the vignette studies judge that Erica was healthy even when she engaged in what is commonly referred to as an "unhealthy" lifestyle: some English speakers might have a negative concept of health.

Huber et al. (2016) provide further support to the claim that not everyone endorse a positive concept of health. They examined whether medical practitioners and lay people endorse the positive characterization of health called "Positive Health," which identifies health with adaptability (Huber et al. 2011, 1: "the ability to adapt and self-manage in the face of social, physical and emotional challenges"; see van der Linden and Schermer 2024a for the history of this movement). Participants were presented with the core ideas of Positive Health and were asked whether they agreed with them. (Notice that as discussed in Section 1, the methodology of Huber et al. (2016) differs substantially from the ones employed in the experimental-philosophy studies presented above: it asks people explicit theoretical questions about health instead of examining how people use the concept of health.) Of particular importance in the present context is the fact that a substantial minority of participants agreed with statements such as "This description [referring to the core ideas of Positive Health] seems to make actual disease unimportant" (31.2%), "This is too broad, it is about life and not about health" (30.9%), and "For me, health is primarily the absence of disease" (22.0%). Furthermore, participants disagreed about the importance of various dimensions "as being part of health" (Huber et al. 2016; Figures 1 and 2): in particular, policymakers and researchers appeared to judge "quality of life," "social and societal participation," and "daily functioning" as less important than the groups of patients, health care providers, and public health actors, suggesting again variation in the acceptance of a positive characterization of health. Huber et al. (2016, 8) summarize their findings as follows:

> all stakeholder groups considered bodily functions to represent health, whereas judgements about the other dimensions differed significantly between groups. Patients considered all six dimensions [i.e., the dimensions identified by the Positive Health movement] as almost equally important, thus preferring a broad concept of health, whereas policymakers as well as healthcare providers (and among the latter especially physicians) assessed health in a more narrow and biomedical way.

On the other hand, despite this variation, no group (viz. patients, policymakers, healthcare providers, etc.) rejected entirely the importance of "quality of life," "social and societal participation," and "daily functioning" for health (see also van Heteren et al.'s (2023) semi-structured interview of Dutch frontline health professionals): they just judged them less important. This finding suggests that no group endorsed a purely negative conception of health; rather, each group embraced a somewhat different positive conception of health.

Demographic factors appear to influence people's concepts of health (e.g., d'Houtaud and Field 1984; Calnan and Johnson 1985; Peersman et al. 2012; Stronks et al. 2018; De Jong et al. 2020). d'Houtaud and Field (1984) asked French participants to explain what health meant to them and they found variation across socioeconomic groups: lower socioeconomic status people were more likely to embrace a negative conception of health. (Note again how their methodology differs from the studies reported above.) Stronks et al. (2018) used the methodology of concept mapping (see also De Jong et al. 2020): statements about health were generated by Dutch participants before being classified as a function of their similarity (e.g., "belong together in a way that makes sense to you"); clusters of statements were then computationally produced. Participants were divided into three groups depending on their socioeconomic status (high, medium, and low socioeconomic statuses). Negativism failed to describe how these groups conceptualize health (see also Simon et al. 2005; De Jong et al. 2020; van Heteren et al. 2023): for all of them, health included many other characteristics (experiences such as "being comfortable in your skin" and rest, capabilities, habits, and practices). The clusters identified for each group also overlapped substantially: all socioeconomic groups had clusters related to the absence of disease, to health-related behavior, and to social relations, to name only three. These similarities were accompanied by differences. For instance, in line with the older findings reported by d'Houtaud and Field (1984), negative statements were among the statements judged most important by people from a low socioeconomic status (e.g., "Having no stress" and "Having no chronic disease"); capabilities were among the statements judged most important by people from high and medium socioeconomic statuses (e.g., being able to cope).

2.4 Mental Health

We questioned earlier the scope of the lay rejection of negativism. In particular, one might wonder whether there is a difference between physical and mental health: is being mentally healthy just not suffering from any mental disorder? In a study described in greater detail in Section 3, Varga and Latham (2024b) examined whether four factors influence the application of the concepts of health and disorder to the mind: group valuation (whether a condition is positively or negatively valued by the community the vignette's character belongs to), individual valuation (whether a condition is positively or negatively valued by this character), outcome (whether the condition benefits the character or not), and its source (what causes this condition). The vignettes participants read (which we review at greater length in Section 3) described the condition of a character, which varied according to these four factors (resulting in 16 possible different vignettes). After reading a vignette, participants were asked to rate on a 7-point scale their agreement with two statements: "In this scenario, Katie is healthy" and "In this scenario, Katie has a mental disorder."

Varga and Latham found that while judgments about health and disorder are both affected by outcome and individual valuation, in the case of disorder, but not in the case of health, it is because outcome and individual valuation affect judgments about whether the condition is a dysfunction, which in turn, together with the source of the disorder, affect judgments about whether it is a disorder; in the case of health, the factors outcome and individual valuation (but not the source of the condition) influence participants' judgments directly. Figure 7 summarizes this difference.

These findings extend the conclusion drawn previously about the lay concept of health: in the psychological domain too, the concept of health is not just the absence of disorder. They also suggest that the concept of mental health has a subjective dimension (perhaps in line with the position developed by Nordenfelt 1995, 2007): whether someone has a positive attitude toward their own condition influences whether that condition is thought to be healthy or not. To caricature a bit, if a schizophrenic patient values hearing voices or otherwise unusual hallucinatory experiences, she is more likely to be thought to be psychologically healthy (see, e.g., Lorente-Rovira et al. 2020 for a description of people with schizophrenia displaying positive hallucinations). How significant this subjectivity is remains a topic for future inquiry: would one be healthy if one values one's condition, even if it is harmful according to some measures? Is the significance of subjectivity dismissed when the positive valuation of a medical condition such as schizophrenia is itself viewed as resulting from the condition itself? What's more, do medical practitioners acknowledge the significance of people's own valuations? They do acknowledge their significance at least for psychological disorders (in contrast to psychological health). For instance, according to the *Diagnostic and Statistical Manual of Mental Disorders* (DSM-5; APA 2013) a woman can only be classified as having a Female Sexual Interest/Arousal Disorder if she experiences "distress" because of her condition (Varga, Latham, and Stegenga 2025).

The findings just discussed suggest that the concept of mental health might also have an objective dimension since health judgments were influenced by whether the condition's consequences were positive or negative. We note however that this factor is not unambiguously objective since

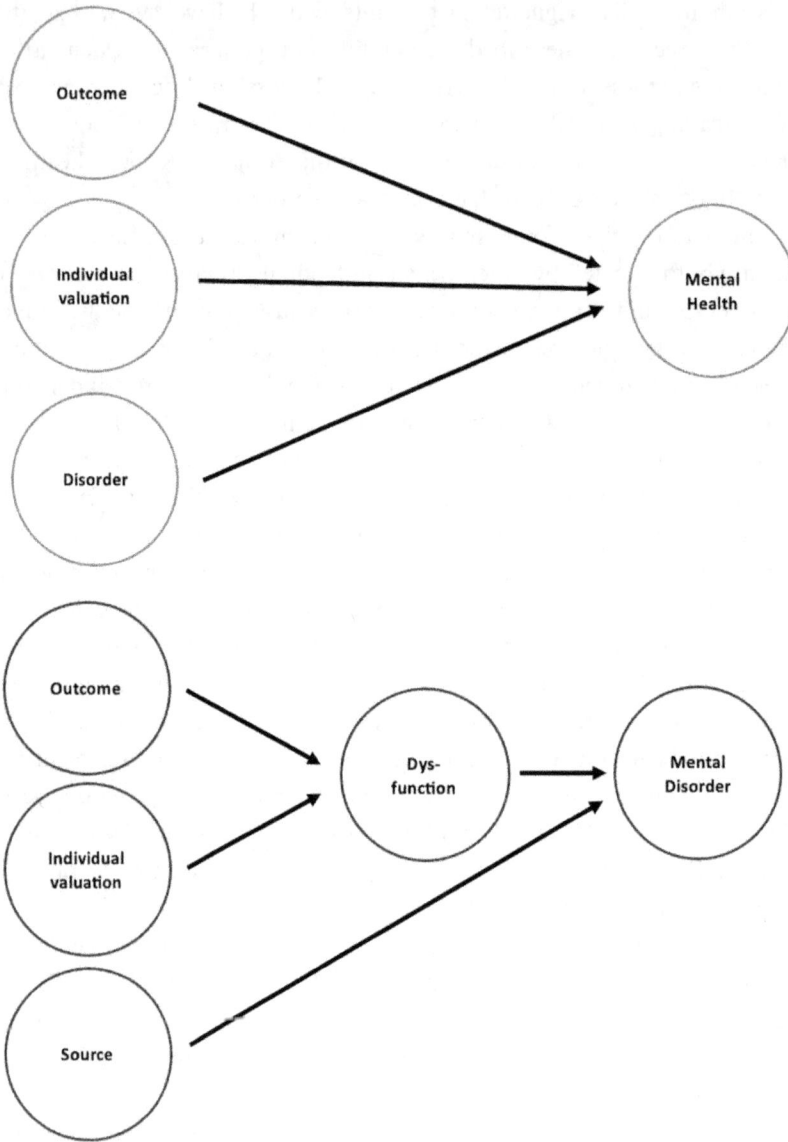

Figure 7 Two Different Causal Pathways for the Concepts of Mental Health and Mental Disorder

people might assume that the positive consequences are those actually valued and the bad consequences are those disvalued by the person experiencing the condition.

Since the conclusions drawn are based on only a small number of studies, focusing on a limited set of symptoms, it is reasonable to question whether these results generalize more broadly. While more studies are clearly

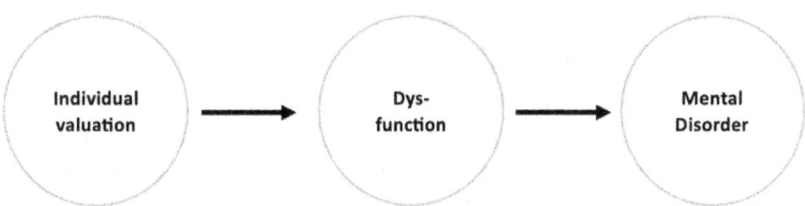

Figure 8 The Causal Pathway for the Concept of Health Applied to Sexual Interest/Arousal Disorder

needed to confirm and extend these findings, a recent study represents a first step in this direction. Varga, Latham, and Stegenga (2025) examined the issue with the example of Sexual Interest/Arousal Disorder. The results are similar, although not identical, to the ones reported earlier. The patient's assessment of her own condition – whether she values it, minds it, or is neutral – did matter for assessing whether someone manifesting the symptoms of Sexual Interest/Arousal Disorder is healthy: if a person does not mind, they are more likely to be judged healthy. However, this impact was mediated by the ascription of dysfunction, perhaps because the condition is partly thought of as being "physical" (Figure 8).

2.5 The Concept of Health

We now have a better, although still partial, understanding of the lay concept of health. Currently, health, as understood by lay people, or at least by many Westerners (we will drop this qualification in what follows), is not just the absence of diseases. It appears that someone can have some chronic disease and still be healthy, provided that they are asymptomatic, even if they are at substantial risk of experiencing symptoms. Furthermore, judgments about mental health are influenced by considerations that differ from those influencing judgments about psychological disorders. In being more than just the absence of diseases (if not in detail), the lay concept of health is similar to the characterizations of health endorsed by the World Health Organization and, much more recently, by the Positive Health movement in the Netherlands (already mentioned earlier), as well as to those characterizations of "positive health" embodied in remedial medicine and in the aspects of everyday life that go under the heading "health and wellness."

The findings reviewed in this section also allow us to be more precise about the relation between disease and health for lay people: it is not necessary to be disease-free to be healthy; nor is it necessary to be fully shielded from the risk of experiencing clinical symptoms to be healthy. We speculate that the absence of symptoms might however be associated with health: the fewer symptoms and the less severe they are, the healthier someone should appear. For instance, someone with asthma or herpes simplex might be judged healthy when she is asymptomatic, but not when they are undergoing an asthma attack or have a blister on their lips. Further empirical work must confirm this speculation. We also wonder whether the lay concept of health distinguishes chronic diseases from non-chronic diseases. Finally, while evidence is unfortunately limited in this respect, it appears that physicians' and medical students' concept of health might be quite similar to lay people's.

Furthermore, health, as lay people understand it, also involves having a particular lifestyle, including having a "healthy" diet and engaging in "healthy" physical activities. Some activities that are currently negatively valenced (but were not always – think of Marlboro Man), such as smoking and having little sleep, are also related to poor health by lay people: even if one has no disease, engaging in these activities is sufficient to be judged unhealthy. The prominence of lifestyle in the positive concept of health might be a development of the 1980s. In addition to the absence of symptoms, we view these activities and habits as the second aspect of the current concept of health. A fully healthy individual is an asymptomatic person, who engages in a range of activities and habits, as well as refrains from other activities and habits. This concept seems to have a prototypical structure, where activities typical of healthy individuals are built into a concept. (A concept has a prototype structure just in case it represents the typical characteristics of the members of its extension, and leads people to perceive some of these members as better or worse instances of the concept.) If this is correct, then we would expect lay people to find people increasingly healthy as a function of how many typical properties they happen to possess: an asymptomatic individual who exercises and has a balanced diet would thus be judged to be healthier than an asymptomatic individual who has a balanced diet but does not exercise.

Just like physical health, mental health is not just the absence of mental disorders. At least for lay people, mental health also involves a subjective and evaluative component: mental health depends on the perspective of the individual, on how she is experiencing and valuing her own condition. Mental and physical health may or may not differ in this respect. Evidence discussed in Section 3 suggests that the lay concept of disease is not subjective in this way (but see van der Linden and Schermer 2024b for interview-based evidence that some medical practitioners recognize the importance of patients' valuation even in the case of somatic diseases), but the concept of physical health could be partly subjective and evaluative even if the concept of disease is not.

2.6 Philosophical Implications

We do not take surveys of lay people or even medical practitioners to provide direct answers to the questions philosophers of medicine are interested in. The only exception is when philosophers of medicine make explicit claims about the concepts of disease, health, or disorder held by laypeople or medical practitioners. Rather, we view the study of the lay concept of health (or disease, or disorder) as providing evidence that can be brought to bear, via philosophical argumentation, on philosophical debates about health and disease in the philosophy of medicine (e.g., by providing constraint on how to reform these concepts or by providing evidence relevant to assess whether a philosophical theory of health and disease has changed the topic).

Most obviously, our findings bear on negativism about health in the philosophy of medicine (e.g., Boorse 1977). To the extent that negativism is about either lay people's or medical practitioners' *concept* of health, it is decisively undermined by the findings reviewed in this section. (Even when variation is found, neither patients as a group nor any group of medical practitioners endorsed a negative concept of health, although *some* individuals did report identifying health with just the absence of disease.) But perhaps negativism is not meant to be describing *these* concepts: perhaps it is meant to describe the concept of a narrow sliver of medical practitioners, perhaps researchers in the biomedical sciences (e.g., oncologists), or perhaps pathologists (as in the work of Boorse). If negativism is to be so understood, then the crucial issue is the lack of evidence supporting it: why believe that this group endorses negativism? (Huber et al. 2016 report evidence of variation between patients and some medical practitioners, but practitioners themselves did not embrace a purely negative concept of health.)

But perhaps negativism is not meant to be understood as a claim about what anyone's concept of health is like. Perhaps it is a claim about how the concept of health *should* be understood: it is a proposal to reform or engineer that concept (on engineering in the philosophy of medicine, see Section 1; see also Schwartz 2007a, 2014; Kukla 2014; Gagné-Julien 2024; Lalumera 2025; and about health in particular, see Huber et al. 2011; van der Linden and Schermer 2024b). Engineering proposals should be assessed not by their accuracy in describing existing concepts but by their capacity to fulfill various epistemic or ethical goals (Machery 2017). On the other hand, as we argued in Section 1, current concepts do constrain, more or less loosely, the acceptability of engineering proposals about these concepts; Carnap (1962), for instance, included similarity to the concept to be explicated as one of his four criteria of evaluation of candidate explications. The trouble, then, is that by differing so much from the current positive concept of health, a purely negative concept wouldn't be able to play many of the roles that the current lay concept, centered around asymptomaticity and prototypical "healthy" activities and habits, happens to play. It wouldn't be able to guide people's choice of activities and habits, except when those are risk factors for diseases, a substantial narrowing of what we currently use the concept of health to do. It wouldn't cast any light on what remedial medicine is aiming at doing (Nordenfelt 2001). Thus, while a purely negative concept of health could have its utility, first such utility would have to be demonstrated, not merely stipulated, and second the negative concept wouldn't really replace the current positive concept of health; it would rather coexist with it. In addition, a negative concept of health could endanger communication between medical practitioners using this concept and the lay public, committed as it is to a positive concept of health. Perhaps more importantly, if these two concepts diverge, then public health policies aiming at addressing health understood negatively could be challenged on the ground that citizens would not judge these policies to be really about health and that the legitimacy of policies depends on how citizens view them (see also Varga et al. 2024).

If engineering is the right approach to the concept of health, engineering a principled *positive* concept of health that precisifies the current lay concept might be more fruitful. It is not clear why some typical activities and habits, but not others, are represented by the current concept of health and we have warned philosophers against expecting the pattern of inclusion and exclusion to be principled. Engineering the concept of health so as to make this pattern more principled, but still continuous with the pattern revealed by experimental philosophy, may be a modest, but promising engineering project. (We will have more to say about engineering below.) There are also several competing positive characterizations of health on offer among philosophers of medicine and medical practitioners, some focused on well-being (e.g., the 1948 characterization offered by the World Health Organization), others on adaptability (e.g., Canguilhem 1966; *Lancet* editorial 2009; Huber et al. 2011), and yet others on capabilities (e.g., Venkatapuram 2011; Mitchell and Alexandrova 2021). How similar these characterizations are to the lay concept of health and how easy it would be to transition from the lay concept of health to them could be a criterion for choosing among these alternatives (perhaps one criterion among several).

Finally, negativism might be understood as a theory of *health* itself and not as a theory of the concept of health. From this point of view, whether it correctly describes the lay concept of health (or for that matter, medical practitioners') does not matter, exactly as a chemical theory of water is not hostage to describing the lay concept of water. We acknowledge that this is a possible understanding of negativism, but we question why we should care about health so understood. What is the philosophical or scientific benefit of singling out this form of health? (This concern is similar to the one we expressed above about the motivation for viewing negativism as an engineering proposal.)

Beyond the debate about negativism, our findings also bear on the scope of medicine and thus on the role of medical professionals. One could propose that the proper scope of medicine is to be restricted to diseases and psychiatric disorders, but this restriction would exclude from medicine a substantial part of what is currently called "medicine" as well as part of the research that goes on in medical schools. Let's assume rather that promoting health, in particular as understood by lay people, falls within the purview of medicine – concerns about overmedicalization or demedicalization duly noted. If this is the case, medicine should partly be concerned with treating the symptomatology of diseases and with assessing the practices and habits associated with health. (Arguably, a large part of medicine is already doing just that.) Assessing these practices and habits should go hand in hand with the kind of conceptual engineering project we have recommended: medical practitioners and philosophers of medicine should identify the activities and habits that a reformed positive concept of health should associate with health in a principled manner.

Lay people take into account people's own evaluative perspective on their conditions when they assess whether they are psychologically healthy. A purely objective understanding of mental health would thus give rise to miscommunication between mental health practitioners and the lay public (for some qualitative, interview-based evidence that medical professionals are attuned to this concern, see van der Linden and Schermer 2024a). Here too, empirical findings can underlie promising conceptual engineering projects. To promote efficient communication and, perhaps more important, to respect patients' autonomy, mental health practitioners' concept of mental health should be reformed if it does not give sufficient room to people's own perspective; conversely, lay people's concept of mental health could specify whether and when people's evaluative perspective on their own condition can be contested by mental health practitioners.

Finally, we noted earlier that conceptual engineering should be assessed by considering either epistemic or ethical goals. The latter deserve mention here: one can have concerns with a positive concept of health on ethical or political grounds. Varga and colleagues (2024) have argued that positive conceptions of health risk violating a principle of neutrality by promoting a particular conception of a good life. In addition, a positive conception of health built around an unprincipled subset of activities and habits currently associated with "health" might result in a morally problematic devaluing of "unhealthy" people, that is, people who do not engage in these activities or do not have these habits: if a healthy life leads to a good life, then "unhealthy" people do something wrong; their behavior is less than admirable. What's more, the lay concept of health might be found to be individualistic and to neglect the role of the environment: being healthy as the folk understand it might be more a matter of individuals doing the right thing than of their environment and of the social constraints bearing on them. The assessment of Positive Health in Huber et al. (2016) suggests that many are aware of this aspect of positive characterization of health, although they might in fact approve of it: 30% of participants agreed with the statement "It focuses on individual responsibility." The lay concept might also reflect the ideological influence of higher socioeconomic groups, reflecting their values to the detriment of the rest of society. The empirical study of the concept of health might thus reveal some potential ethical concerns with our lay concept of health that might call for revision.

3 Disease and Dysfunction

While the previous section focuses on the concept of health, this section synthesizes the current evidence from experimental philosophy about the lay concept of disease. We first consider the *evaluative issue*: whether the concept of disease is evaluative or not. Evidence to date, perhaps surprisingly, suggests that the concept of disease is nonevaluative, and might even align with naturalism about disease. We then examine whether the concept of dysfunction is evaluative or not. This issue is important because, as discussed in Section 1, nonevaluative concepts of disease are typically understood in terms of dysfunction, but if people conceive of dysfunction in evaluative terms, then, ultimately, how people conceive of disease will be evaluative too. The nuanced and surprising picture that will emerge is that while people tend to understand physical diseases and dysfunctions in a nonevaluative manner, the same may not be true of mental disorders and dysfunctions.

3.1 The Impact of Dysfunction and Evaluation on the Lay Concepts of Disease and Disorder

Across a series of experiments, Machery (2023) examined the lay concept of disease by assessing how English-speaking participants' disease judgments were influenced by whether a condition was typical, dysfunctional, and disvalued. One of the eight vignettes seen by participants in Experiment 1 read as follows (numbers have been added to the vignette to help identify the factors being tested next):

> As a result of a genetic mutation on chromosome 17[1], one person out of 20 living on the large island of Corsica in the Mediterranean Sea[2], South of France grow up with purple eyes. The purple color of their eyes prevents them from seeing colors as well as other islanders[3]. Islanders in Corsica dislike these people's eye color[4]."

Each part of this vignette represents one factor that has been thought to influence people's disease judgments. The text picked out by [1] describes the *condition's source and type*: here a genetic mutation affecting the visual system. This factor was varied across vignettes, which referred to bacteria affecting the auditory system and to an environmental factor (viz. nuclear reactor) affecting the musculoskeletal system. The text picked out by [2] describes the *typicality* of the condition: here the condition has low typicality, with high typicality cases referring to three in every four persons. The text picked out by [3] describes whether the condition is *dysfunctional*: here the condition is dysfunctional because it prevents people from seeing colors; in no-dysfunction cases the condition did not impact a person's vision at all. Finally, the text picked out by [4] describes whether the condition is *disvalued*: here, the condition is disvalued by the group, but in non-disvalued cases, people do not mind the condition.

After reading the vignette, participants were asked their level of agreement with the statement "These people's purple eyes are a disease." Participants were able to respond using a 7-point scale that ranged from 1 (strongly agree) to 7 (strongly disagree). The results of Study 1 are shown in Figure 9.

As is evident from Figure 9, dysfunction was the *only* factor found to have any significant influence on disease judgments: people agreed more that a condition was a disease when it involved having a visual, auditory, or musculoskeletal dysfunction. In contrast, there was no evidence that the group's evaluation mattered at all: disease judgments were the same regardless of whether the group disliked the condition or not. In addition, there was no evidence that either condition source and type or condition typicality mattered to people's disease judgments (although the former was not examined systematically).

This pattern of results was later replicated by Varga, Latham, and Stegenga (2025) with more realistic conditions than those used by Machery (2023): low sexual desire. Varga and colleagues also found *no* evidence that how *individuals themselves* (in contrast to the *society* they belong to) evaluate their own condition has any effect on disease judgments: disease

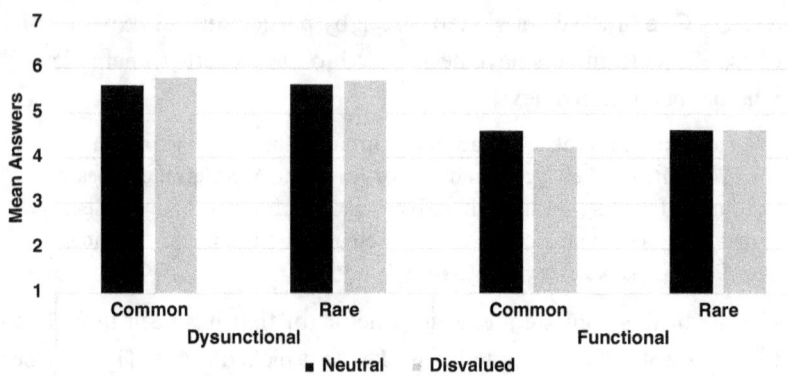

Figure 9 Results in Study 1 of Machery 2023. Participants' disease judgments (1 = strongly agree purple eyes is a disease) as a function of typicality, valuation, and dysfunctionality.

judgments were the same regardless of whether the person who had the condition disliked it and thought that it was harmful or not. Furthermore, the extent to which people judge a condition to be a disease depends on the extent to which they judge this condition to involve a dysfunction (Varga, Latham, and Machery 2025c). Noteworthily, Varga, Latham, and Stegenga's (2025) results show that the impact of dysfunction as well as the lack of impact of personal and group valuation are not limited to physical conditions, but also extend to psychological conditions such as low sexual desire. Personal and group valuations could influence disorder judgments in the case of psychological conditions that are less physical or organic, although evidence is so far lacking regarding this issue.

The impact of dysfunction on judgments about a range of mental disorders is relatively well established. Kirk et al. (1999) were interested in whether *social workers* reliably distinguish between people having a mental disorder and people responding in what might be considered to be an ordinary fashion to negative environments. Participants were presented with a case describing someone meeting the description of having a conduct disorder according to the DSM-IV. They were then told either that this person's conduct was the result of an internal dysfunction or of a negative environment. Participants were significantly more likely to judge that someone had a mental disorder when the case was described as being a result of an internal dysfunction compared to cases in which only the conduct disorder was described, or when the conduct was described as being the result of the environment (a pattern subsequently replicated in two follow-up studies: Wakefield et al. 1999; Pottick et al. 2003; for overview, see Wakefield 2021). So, dysfunction matters not only for lay people without any background in medicine but also for people at the periphery of the medical world, such as social workers. Whether and how it matters for medical professionals is unknown, but we expect that it would.

Kirk et al. (1999), along with follow-up studies, systematically examined the influence of a condition's source (for disorders) that Machery (2023) only explored non-systematically (for physical conditions). Their findings suggest that the contrast between a genetic etiology and a social etiology matters for mental health disorders. Béghin and Faucher (2023) built on these findings by examining a wide range of disorders. Consistent with Wakefield and colleagues, they found that cases of attention deficit hyperactivity disorder and major depression disorder that are described as resulting from an internal dysfunction were significantly more likely to be judged to be a mental disorder than both symptom-only cases (viz. fulfilling the DSM-5 criteria necessary for diagnosis), and cases where the atypical conduct was described as being the result of a negative environment. Put another way, when the choices and behaviors characteristic of certain mental disorders can be explained by environmental factors, people are less likely to judge that the evaluation target has a mental disorder than when they can be explained by a dysfunction.

Related results have also been found by Varga and colleagues (Varga and Latham 2024b; Varga, Latham, and Stegenga 2025). They observed that both low sexual desire and a hypothetical mental condition that prevented deliberation were less likely to be judged to be mental disorders when described as being the result of social as opposed to genetic causes. Interestingly, mental disorder ascriptions were influenced not only by the cause of the condition but also by how the condition is causally intervened upon. Consistent with the results just described, De Block et al. (2023) observed that a mental condition characterized by "attentional issues" and by "easily being scared by new situations" was more likely to be considered a mental disorder when described as being the result of genetics as opposed to either bullying or nonsocial environmental causes. They also observed that when the attentional issues and fear were described as being treated by a psychopharmacological intervention as opposed to an environmental intervention, people were more likely to consider the condition a mental disorder. This latter finding suggests that people make the (perhaps mistaken) inference that if a condition is being treated pharmacologically, then it is more likely to be the result of an internal, biological, and perhaps genetic problem. Future research should examine what it is about treatment options that influence people's judgments about disorder.

These findings can be viewed as supporting the hypothesis that lay people are committed to some form of "folk naturalism" about physical diseases and mental disorders (Machery 2023). Whether someone has a disease or a disorder does not depend on her own evaluation of her condition or how her group views this condition. (It remains unclear whether this is true of all psychological disorders.) Rather, whether someone has a disease or a disorder depends on whether this condition interferes with "normal" (in some unspecified sense) functioning and is judged to be a dysfunction. Of course, this stands in an interesting tension with the finding that dysfunction *itself* might be partially an evaluative notion – a tension that will require further studies to fully understand. Moreover, we speculate that the contrast between "social factors" and "genetic factors" is related to the role of dysfunction in disease and disorder judgments: lay people might be more likely to think that a condition is due to a dysfunction when it results from a genetic factor than from a social factor. Further research needs to examine this speculation.

3.2 The Evaluative Issue

So what are the implications of the results described so far? Recall the *evaluative issue* from Section 1: is the concept of disease evaluative or not? In philosophy of medicine there are three predominant responses: *naturalism, normativism,* and *hybridism*. According to naturalism, the concept of disease is not evaluative, whereas according to normativism, it is. Hybridism, as the name suggests, posits that the concept of disease has both nonevaluative and evaluative parts.

The most robust empirical findings to date in XPhiMed are the influence of dysfunction on people's disease and mental disorder judgments (e.g., Wakefield 2021; Béghin and Faucher 2023; Machery 2023; Varga and Latham 2024b; Varga, Latham, and Stegenga 2025; Varga, Latham, and Machery 2025c; but see the discussion of Varga and Latham's (2025) work on dysfunction and disorder discussed below) and the lack of evidence for an effect of individual or group valuation. Bracketing for the moment how people conceive of dysfunction, these findings suggest that people have a (proto-)naturalist concept of disease.

The apparent lack of influence of evaluations on disease judgments is surprising. In response, it might be suggested that there are several concepts in the vicinity of the concept of disease and that hybridism and normativism are providing accounts of those other concepts. However, most straightforward proposals run into further empirical challenges. Many naturalists agree that while the concept of disease is value-free, the concepts of sickness and illness are value-laden and include a negative evaluation of the person's physical or mental state. However, evidence suggests that people do not make a straightforward conceptual distinction between having a disease and being sick. In Section 2, we described the results of a semantic generation task performed by Reuter et al. (2025). When people were asked about the target probe word "sickness," people reported disease symptoms and dysfunctions. If, however, people hold a normative or hybrid concept of sickness, then you might have expected people to report at least some negative evaluations. It is possible that negative evaluations might show up if people had been asked about "illness" instead of "sickness," but if people do not make a distinction between disease and sickness, then it seems unlikely that they would then make a distinction between sickness and illness.

Another possibility trades on the distinction between biological parts and persons. For instance, it might be that while the concept of disease applies to parts of persons, the concepts of sickness and illness apply to persons. Someone with a condition that is asymptomatic because of some treatment might correctly count as having a disease, without being sick or ill. In contrast, someone who is, for instance, intoxicated might correctly count as being sick or ill, without counting as having a disease. Researchers have perhaps failed to find evidence of evaluations influencing disease judgments because evaluations have little relevance to whether some biological part counts as having a disease; nevertheless, they might matter for whether a person counts as being sick or ill. However, there is again evidence that people do not make a distinction between biological parts and persons when issuing disease judgments: Varga, Machery, and Latham (2025b) found no difference between person-level and subpersonal-level disease judgments.

3.3 Troubles for Naturalism? Evaluation and the Concept of Disorder

Varga and Latham (2024b), already discussed, observed that participants were more likely to judge that the condition was a mental disorder when it brought about negative outcomes rather than positive outcomes. Positive outcomes were characterized as being whatever it is that fulfilled the agent's conception of the good life, well-being, and long-term happiness, whereas negative outcomes were characterized as whatever frustrates it. Thus, mental disorder judgments might turn on whether the condition contributes to or frustrates subjective well-being. This is consistent with how judgments about psychological health seem to depend on the perspective of the person with the condition, as we saw in Section 2.

Varga and Latham (2024b) also observed that whether the outcome is good or bad and how a patient evaluates their own condition influenced whether a condition counts as a dysfunction at all: participants were more likely to judge that the condition was a dysfunction when it brought about negative outcomes (perhaps unsurprisingly) and when it was negatively evaluated by the patient (Figure 7). The influence of patients' evaluation on mental disorder and on dysfunction judgments shows that naturalism about the concepts of disease and disorder we just discussed cannot be the whole story, at least for the concept of mental disorder. If evaluations influence dysfunction judgments, then people might not understand disease in purely naturalistic terms after all. We need to take a step back and look more closely at how people conceive of dysfunction.

3.4 The Lay Concept of Dysfunction: Valuation and Selected Function

Philosophers of medicine have devoted less attention to how lay people understand dysfunction compared to how they understand disease. Most seem to view the concept of biological function as technical and theoretical (but see Wakefield and Conrad 2020, who maintain that the selected effects account, according to which biological dysfunction occurs when an internal part fails to perform the role that it was selected for by natural selection, is continuous with the lay understanding of function): if the concept of biological function is indeed theoretical, one may justly wonder what role lay judgments could ever play in philosophical discussions of function; one might also wonder whether there is even a lay concept of dysfunction. While these concerns are certainly respectable, we will set them aside here; instead, we describe some studies that have taken up the question of how lay people conceive of dysfunction.

In their study, Varga and Latham (2025) presented participants with a vignette describing someone who was either infertile or had ADHD; that person either positively or negatively evaluated their condition. If lay people's understanding of dysfunction is value neutral, then what someone thinks about their own condition should not influence dysfunction judgments. The infertility vignette read as follows (the negative version of vignette is shown in square brackets):

Infertility (Globozoospermia):
38-year old Adam contacts his doctor to get a vasectomy (male surgical sterilization), because he does not want to have more children./[38-year old Adam contacts his doctor to get a fertility check-up, because he wants to have more children.]

Before going further, the doctor orders several tests. The tests reveal that while Adam has no other health concerns, he has grown infertile due to Globozoospermia (also known as round-headed sperm syndrome) – a condition characterized by the presence of sperm with a round head, which makes it difficult or impossible for the sperm to penetrate and fertilize an egg, leading to male infertility. Globozoospermia is otherwise harmless and symptomless.

Learning about his condition, Adam is relieved and pleased that he does not need the vasectomy. The doctor concludes the consultation and does not suggest any treatments aimed at restoring his fertility./[Learning about his condition, Adam is sad and distressed that he needs medical treatment. The doctor suggests a treatment aimed at restoring his fertility.]

In contrast, the ADHD vignette read as follows:

ADHD:
38-year-old Adam has a background in tech and project management. He has always deeply desired a job in a slow-paced environment that lets him focus entirely on one task at a time, feeling the thrill of immersing himself deeply into a single project. He firmly believes that he would flourish in such an environment, and that this type of work would genuinely enable him to unlock his creativity and potential./[38-year-old Adam has a background in tech and project management. He has always deeply desired a job in a fast-paced environment that lets him jump from one task to another, feeling the thrill of juggling multiple projects. He firmly believes that he would flourish in such an environment, and that this type of work would genuinely enable him to unlock his creativity and potential.]

As part of a career development program, Adam undergoes a series of psychological assessments with a reputable psychiatrist. He's diagnosed with ADHD, primarily of the inattentive subtype. This condition means that he tends to overlook details in fast-paced environments and struggle with task-switching. However, when deeply engaged, he can experience "hyper-focus" – a state of heightened, focused attention that individuals with ADHD frequently report – allowing him to become intensely engrossed in one task, often leading to exceptional results.

Upon receiving his ADHD diagnosis, Adam feels a sense of relief. He does not mind having this condition; in fact, he believes it aligns perfectly with his dream job in a slow-paced environment that requires focus on one task at a time. He now realizes that his dream job not only harmonizes well with his natural predispositions but also provides the kind of environment where he can thrive and excel. Adam informs the psychiatrist that he is not interested in any medical treatment, believing there is no need to alter his attention and cognitive style. The psychiatrist respects his decision and offers guidance on optimizing his strengths./[Upon receiving his ADHD diagnosis, Adam feels sad and distressed. He really minds having this condition; indeed, he believes it makes it impossible for him to pursue his dream job in a fast-paced environment that requires quick task-switching. He now realizes that his ideal job is not only entirely misaligned with his natural predispositions but also fails to provide the kind of environment where he can thrive or excel. Adam informs the psychiatrist that he wants medical treatment, believing there is a need to alter his attention and cognitive style. The psychiatrist recommends a blend of behavioural therapy and medication to better manage his symptoms.]

After reading a vignette, participants were asked their level of agreement with the statement "Given the facts of the scenario, it would be correct to say that Adam's reproductive system/attention has a dysfunction". Participants responded on a 7-point scale, ranging from 1 (strongly agree) to 7 (strongly disagree). The results are shown in Figure 10.

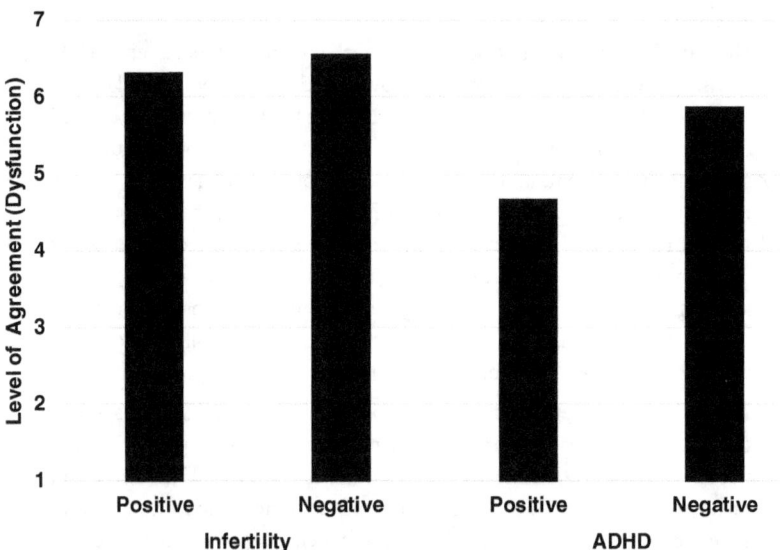

Figure 10 Interaction Effect between Condition and Patient Valuation in Varga and Latham (2025). For infertility, there is no difference in dysfunction judgments between positive and negative patient evaluation. In contrast, for ADHD, dysfunction judgments are higher when negatively evaluated by the patient.

Their findings were striking. First, in the case of infertility, nearly all participants judged that the person had a dysfunction, regardless of how the person viewed their infertility. In contrast, in the case of ADHD, participants were much more likely to judge that the person had a dysfunction when they evaluated their mental condition negatively. Thus, while judgments about dysfunctions for physical conditions appear to be value neutral, dysfunction judgments for mental conditions might not be: how a person evaluates their own mental condition matters for whether we judge their condition to be a dysfunction.

These results about mental disorders are consistent with Kohne et al. (2023). Kohne and colleagues performed a series of semi-structured interviews and thematic analysis to understand what clinicians and patients think mental disorders are. Interestingly, almost no patients or clinicians, especially those with lived experience of a mental health disorder, described biological (brain) dysfunctions. Instead, common to both patients and clinicians was the theme of functional impairment. Functional impairment is based on a much broader notion of function and is concerned with a person's capacity to fulfill their social, societal, and professional roles. As they quote one psychiatrist, "I think ultimately you have to start looking at um… How someone's functioning improves […] in the work area, in the relational area." In Varga and Latham (2025), Adam in the positive ADHD condition judges that he can fulfill his dream job, whereas in the negative ADHD condition he judges that he cannot. In both cases Adam might have a psychophysiological dysfunction, but his attention is only judged to be dysfunctional when it frustrates his professional role.

Recently, Béghin and Faucher (2023) examined whether dysfunction judgments were sensitive to whether symptomatic behaviors were the result of an evolved mechanism doing what it was selected for. Surprisingly, they found that conditions meeting the descriptions of ADHD, major depressive disorder, and anorexia nervosa were *not* judged to be dysfunctions when these conditions were the result of evolved mechanisms, just as the selected effects account of function would predict (but see Braddon-Mitchell et al. ms who find contrary evidence for a somatic disease). Thus, when information about underlying mechanisms and their teleological function is provided, dysfunction and mental disorder judgments track the presence or absence of an internal dysfunction, understood in teleological terms, even when the symptomatic behaviors being described undoubtedly constitute a functional impairment (Kohne et al. 2023). Antisocial personality was the only case where no effect of a teleological function was observed, perhaps because people do not find plausible adaptationist accounts about how a mechanism that favors antisocial personality disorder could have been historically selected for in a social species like ours.

3.5 Is the Concept of Dysfunction Evaluative?

Naturalist and hybridist accounts of disease focus on nonevaluative facts about biological dysfunctions (Section 1). Functions on the Bio-Statistical Theory are characterized in statistical terms: normal functioning consists in the statistically normal contribution of an internal part to survival or reproduction in a reference class. The harmful dysfunction analysis characterizes function in evolutionary terms: a function is the historical role that an internal part of an organism was naturally selected to perform (for other accounts of functions in the philosophy of medicine and biology, see, e.g., Griffiths and Matthewson 2018; Garson 2019; Christie et al. 2023).

One of the main discoveries to emerge from the experimental philosophy of medicine is that what it means to have a dysfunction – the concept of dysfunction if you will – appears to differ in the context of somatic diseases and of mental disorders (but see the following caveat). Varga and Latham's (2025) findings suggest that the lay concept of dysfunction is nonevaluative when it comes to somatic diseases. Thus, naturalism appears to be capturing how lay people think of somatic diseases: evaluation influences neither indirectly (via judgments about dysfunction) nor directly lay judgments about disease.

The situation appears different for disorders. According to narrow normativism (Section 1), whether a condition counts as a dysfunction is irrelevant to whether it counts as a disease; by contrast, wide normativists agree with naturalists and hybridists that there is a connection between disease and dysfunction, but hold that our concept of dysfunction too is value-laden. Varga and Latham's (2025) findings suggest that the lay concept of dysfunction is evaluative when it comes to mental disorders, providing some support for wide normativism.

But which nonevaluative concept of dysfunction is most aligned with the dysfunction judgments made by lay people in relation to diseases and disorders? Displaying the symptoms of major depressive disorder and anorexia nervosa is *not* sufficient for having a mental dysfunction when the mechanism that causes the symptomatic behaviors is doing what it is selected for (Béghin and Faucher 2023); rather, fulfilling the role associated with past historical selection seems to be sufficient for being functional, in line with a selected effects account.

One might wonder how the influence of historical selection on dysfunction judgments about disorders fits with the evidence from Varga and Latham (2025) that evaluation also influences lay judgments about the dysfunctional nature of mental conditions. We speculate that for mental conditions, fulfilling the role associated with past historical selection is sufficient for being functional, while failing to fulfill it is necessary, but not sufficient, for being dysfunctional; being disvalued is also a necessary condition for dysfunction.

We should note a possible deflationary explanation of the observed contrast between dysfunction judgments in the context of disorder and disease. This contrast might not happen because people think about disorder and disease differently, but because Varga and Latham (2025) described the physical and mental cases differently. The description of Globozoospermia leaves little doubt that a part of the reproductive system is not doing what it is supposed to; by contrast, the description of ADHD is silent about the existence of an underlying dysfunction. It could be that when it is not clear whether there is any underlying dysfunction, people consider other factors, when making a dysfunction judgment, such as patients' evaluation of their own condition. If this is correct, once it is made explicit that a dysfunction underlies a mental condition, participants should respond just as they do to the Globozoospermia case. By contrast, if dysfunction judgments really differ between disorders and diseases, a condition resulting from some failure to fulfill a selected role should only be judged a disorder when patients disvalue it.

What about other accounts of function? One of the implications of the Bio-Statistical Theory is that as a dysfunction becomes more common, it eventually ceases to be a dysfunction: if everyone possesses condition X, then X cannot be a dysfunction. While many have found this implication deeply problematic, empirical evidence regarding the influence of condition typicality on dysfunction judgments to date has been mixed. As described in Section 1, early studies in experimental philosophy of medicine failed to find any evidence of an effect of typicality on disease judgment, both when the condition affected nearly everyone globally (Varga, Latham, and Machery 2025c) and when it affected nearly everyone in a local population (Machery 2023). In contrast, Braddon-Mitchell et al. (ms) observed that dysfunction judgments for a heart condition were significantly lower when the heart condition affected nearly everyone than when it affected only a few people, just as one would predict if one took seriously the account of function adopted by the Bio-Statistical Theory.

3.6 Framing Disease and Disorder Judgments: Moral Evaluation and Abstract/Concrete Effect

Finally, experimental philosophers of medicine have also examined whether judgments about disease and disorder can be influenced by framing, that is, whether they vary when the relevant conditions are presented in ways that are, at least *prima facie*, irrelevant. For instance, if naturalism is correct of disease and disorder, then moral character is irrelevant and so people are responding in error if they are influenced by moral character. Of course, if normativism is the correct account of disease and disorder, then the fact that people are being influenced by moral character might be just what you would expect. How one evaluates these framing results depends on one's own views regarding the correct account of disease and disorder.

One interesting finding in this area is that evaluations of moral character do appear to influence disease and disorder judgments. In two studies, Varga, Latham, and Machery (2025a, 2025b) examined two competing hypotheses: the *naturalization* and *pathologization* hypotheses. According to the former, negative moral evaluation makes us *less* likely to judge that a condition is a disease: people are typically not responsible for having a disease (diseases, one might think, happen to people) and since we want to be able to blame those whom we morally evaluate negatively, we refrain from viewing their conditions as diseases. So, for instance, perhaps classists do not judge that smoking is a disease because they have a negative evaluation of poor people (who are more likely to smoke; Hiscock et al. 2012) and want to blame them. By contrast, the pathologization hypothesis holds that negative moral evaluation makes us *more* likely to judge that a condition is a disease. That is because diseases are viewed as punishment for someone's having a blameworthy character. Varga and colleagues compared disease judgments between saint-like, evil, and ordinary moral characters experiencing either erectile dysfunction or anxiety. Consistent with the pathologization hypothesis, they observed that participants were more likely to judge *both* the physical and the psychological condition to be diseases for evil characters (Figure 11). Conversely, participants were less likely to judge evil characters with physical and psychological conditions as being healthy.

If the pathologization effect extends to medical professionals, then medical professionals might treat normal variation within a population as being a disease if they happen to evaluate negatively the relevant segment of the population. This in turn raises the risk of overmedicalization. For instance, the historical classification and treatment of homosexuality as a mental disorder might be explained by this effect. Similarly, the

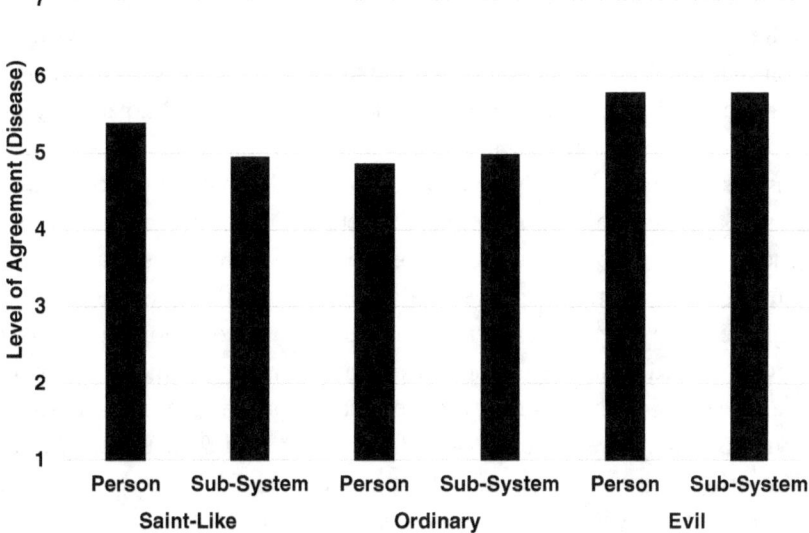

Figure 11 The Pathologization Effect in Varga, Latham, and Machery (2025b). Level of agreement that a person has a disease, or has a subsystem that has a disease is higher when a person has a negative moral character.

temptation today to classify obesity as a disease might be explained by the fact that people evaluate people that are overweight to be bad people.

Relatedly, Lippert-Rasmussen and colleagues (2025, ms) have investigated whether doctors and good friends differ in their moral standing to blame within a healthcare context. One key condition for moral standing is the *relationship condition*: A lacks standing to blame B if A does not stand in a suitable relationship to B. Contrast, for example, someone's standing to blame a total stranger versus their standing to blame a friend. The medical ethics literature has been clear that doctors do *not* have moral standing to blame patients due to the nature of the doctor–patient relationship (e.g., Gunderman 2000; Kelley 2005). Further, moralization in healthcare can negatively impact patient health and hence is seen to run contrary to medicine's primary duty of care (e.g., Stroebe 2011; Ringel and Ditto 2019; Dohle et al. 2022; Kraaijeveld and Jamrozik 2022). Contrary to this, however, Lippert-Rasmussen and colleagues (2025, ms) found that people attribute much higher moral standing to praise and blame to doctors than good friends. This result points to the need for further reflection on what it takes to be suitably related for the purposes of moral standing.

Judgments about whether a condition is a disease also seem to vary depending on whether the condition is described abstractly or concretely.

Braddon-Mitchell and colleagues (ms) wanted to know why people appear to judge certain reproductive conditions that result in infertility to be dysfunctions but not diseases (see Varga and Latham 2025). Building on Varga and Latham (2025), they used the case of Globozoospermia and experimentally manipulated its description in two different ways. First, they manipulated this description to be a dysfunction or not: in the dysfunction condition, participants received the standard characterization of Globozoospermia, whereas in the non-dysfunction condition it was not associated with infertility or any other negative conditions. Second, they manipulated the vignette to be concrete or abstract: in the concrete condition participants were presented with a description of a named person with the condition in the midst of a consultation with a medical doctor, whereas, in the abstract condition, they were presented with just the description of the condition. Surprisingly, people judge that the dysfunctional Globozoospermia is a disease, but only when Globozoospermia is described *abstractly*.

When the influence of abstract and concrete presentations has been observed elsewhere in experimental philosophy, the usual response has been to explain away one of the two incompatible judgments. For instance, people are more likely to offer compatibilist judgments when presented with concrete cases, whereas they are more likely to offer incompatibilist judgments when presented with abstract cases (for a metaanalysis and careful discussion, see Feltz and Cova 2014). In response, some have argued that compatibilist judgments are erroneous because of emotional engagement (e.g., Nichols and Knobe 2007) or intrusive tacit metaphysical commitments (e.g., Nadelhoffer et al. 2020). Others have argued that incompatibilist judgments are erroneous because our concepts of free will and moral responsibility are meant to be used in concrete interpersonal scenarios (e.g., Latham 2019).

Prima facie it is hard to see why describing a condition concretely or abstractly should influence whether it counts as a disease, and it is thus natural to explain away one of the two judgments, as was done elsewhere in experimental philosophy. To keep the connection between dysfunction and disease, naturalists (as well as most hybridists) must interpret disease judgments about Globozoospermia as erroneous when Globozoospermia is described concretely. However, this presents a challenge, as it becomes unclear how naturalists can also maintain that the judgments about other concrete conditions that appear to support naturalism (e.g., Machery 2023) are not equally erroneous.

So where does this leave us? At the beginning of this section we showed that there is mounting evidence that the most important factor for lay disease and disorder judgments is dysfunction. *Prima facie*, such evidence is most consistent with the lay concepts of disease and disorder being aligned with naturalism, assuming that people conceive of dysfunction in nonevaluative terms. However, people appear to make dysfunction judgments differently about physical and mental conditions: while dysfunction judgments about physical conditions are *not* influenced by evaluations, consistent with the lay concept of dysfunction being nonevaluative, dysfunction judgments about mental conditions are influenced by evaluations, suggesting that the lay concept of dysfunction is an evaluative one. Presently, this difference could either track a distinction in kind between physical and mental dysfunction judgments, or be an artifact of how these conditions are often described. More work on the question is called for. Finally, experimental philosophers have investigated whether judgments about disease and disorder can be influenced by framing effects. People are more likely to judge that a condition is a disease when someone has a bad moral character and when described in an abstract manner. Whether these framing effects are judged to be in error or not depends on your own views regarding the correct account of disease and disorder.

4 XPhiMed: Insights and Future Prospects

One impetus for this Element stems from a perceived discrepancy. Debates over the concepts of health and disease in philosophy have gained prominence, driven by a growing recognition of their importance not only for medical research, healthcare, and public health but also for defining what legitimately falls within the scope of medicine. However, there is a growing belief that these debates are making little progress. Existing approaches can account for certain uncontroversial intuitions but fail to offer a comprehensive framework, leading philosophers to cite methodological constraints or argue that these concepts are too anomalous and ambiguous to support a unified theory. XPhiMed responds to this situation and seeks to address the issue by deploying an experimental approach, enhancing traditional conceptual analysis with the integration of empirical methods. As we reach the end of this Element, it is time to ask: what are the main insights that we gained from this endeavor and how could these insights shape the future trajectory of inquiry in the philosophy of medicine?

Before reflecting on the impact on philosophy, let us briefly illustrate how XPhiMed can contribute to fields outside of philosophy. First, XPhiMed can complement traditional qualitative research in health anthropology, sociology, and psychology. For example, this can be achieved by using different experimental methods to systematically test the health "themes" revealed by qualitative studies. Second, by examining the concepts of health and disease and their use in different populations, XPhiMed can inform their more targeted applications in medicine, public health, and policymaking, tailoring communication to specific contexts and demographic groups. For example, it is likely that emphasizing health as "the absence of disease" in public health messaging aimed at groups that view health in terms of lifestyle patterns and social well-being would be less effective. Whether people judge a condition as a disease also seems to depend on whether it is presented concretely or abstractly. If health communication aims to emphasize some condition as a disease, it may be more effective to abstract away from personal details and present the condition in more general terms. Of course, much additional evidence is needed to show that communication effectiveness can be improved in this way and that it leads to tangible health improvements, but the potential is evident.

But how might these insights shape the future trajectories of philosophical inquiry? One way to summarize XPhiMed's contribution and its potential to shape future inquiry is by describing it as helping *reorient* debates. By this, we do not mean anything grandiose. Chalmers (2015) rightly observes that, faced with the limitations of traditional philosophical methods, turning to new approaches (such as experimental philosophy) typically does not lead to straightforward solutions or greater convergence in debates. Instead, it leads to more sophisticated and productive versions of longstanding disagreements. We view XPhiMed's contribution in this manner, by laying the foundation for more refined and productive discussions in three different ways: (1) a *methodological reorientation*, (2) *thematic reorientation*, and (3) the creation of avenues for *new (explanatory) tasks*. Below, we will explain each of these in detail. Importantly, we view this reorientation as *ecumenical*, with the potential to benefit researchers broadly, regardless of their theoretical positions, as outlined in Section 1.

4.1 Methodological Reorientation

The methodological reorientation helps place the debates in the philosophy of medicine on solid empirical footing. Experimental philosophy has had a significant impact in achieving this across several philosophical domains, and there is no obvious reason for its application in the philosophy of medicine to be less impactful. Crucially, researchers across diverse theoretical commitments and perspectives can embrace this reorientation.

Take, for instance, the competing views on why the debates about health and disease have reached an impasse. For those who believe that these debates have stalled because of the limitations of conceptual analysis, XPhiMed's "naturalized" approach offers an improved method. For others who attribute the lack of progress to the complexity and potential irregularity of concepts such as the concepts of health and disease, XPhiMed offers an additional tool to understand this irregularity, which has demonstrated success in other areas of philosophy (e.g., Cushman and Mele 2008).

Or take the competing views about what kind of project we ought to pursue. For those who pursue the descriptive project – whether restricted or unrestricted – and focus on lay concepts of health and disease, XPhiMed helps ensure that their assumptions about common-sense judgments are accurate. For those who maintain that the descriptive project should focus on the concepts held by medical professionals, progress can be made as the experimental method can be just as effectively applied to survey expert perspectives. For those who reject the descriptive project and opt for engineering new concepts of health and disease, XPhiMed can provide valuable support, as the justification for such engineering projects hinges on whether their verdict on existing concepts is descriptively accurate. Moreover, grounding conceptual engineering in experimental philosophy can help ensure that the limitations imposed by common-sense usage are respected, which constrain the acceptability of proposed conceptual revisions.

Of course, the methodological reorientation proposed here can be expanded, and the provision of empirical grounding should not be viewed as confined to experimental vignette-based studies. Many different empirical methods can be deployed to improve philosophical inquiry. For instance, exploring a slightly different avenue, Fulford and Colombo (2004) integrate philosophical analysis with qualitative research to explore the diversity of conceptual frameworks in mental health. Other possibilities include analyzing large datasets of language use (e.g., medical journals, news articles, and social media discussions). Corpus analysis can reveal patterns in how terms such as "health" and "disease" are used, complementing the insights gained from controlled experiments described in this Element.

4.2 Thematic Reorientation

The second way we propose that XPhiMed reorients the debate is by restructuring the research questions themselves. Progress sometimes occurs not by answering old questions but by reframing them, and XPhiMed provides motivation for this shift. It reveals a more complex picture of how the concepts of health and disease function, indicating that greater progress can be made by disentangling certain issues from one another. It is likely that the entanglement of distinct issues has contributed to the emergence of stalemates in the philosophy of medicine. Here, we suggest several ways to approach certain questions on their own terms.

First, and most clearly suggested by our findings, advancement may be better achieved through *separate debates that focus on health and disease individually*. For instance, the findings suggest that the concept of health has a prototypical structure, representing characteristics typically associated with healthy individuals. Importantly, while being free from disease or fully protected from the risk of symptoms may contribute to the judgment that someone is healthy, adopting certain lifestyles with characteristic activities can, on its own, be *sufficient* to support such a judgment. Health is likely viewed as existing on a spectrum, increasing or decreasing based on the number of typical healthy attributes a person possesses. One key lesson is that if we assume that we can fully understand the concept of health by investigating disease alone, we risk overlooking other important features.

Second, the findings also indicate that it would be helpful to diverge from the traditional treatment in the literature and *separate discussions of mental and physical conditions*. Once again, assuming that we can fully understand the concept of mental health or disorder by investigating somatic health or disease alone, or vice versa, risks overlooking important aspects of both. While neither somatic health nor mental health are just the absence of disease or disorder, mental health, unlike physical health, involves a subjective and evaluative component: it depends on the individual's perspective and how they experience and value their own condition. Similarly, the concept of organic disease appears to be naturalistic (value-free), while judgments about mental disorder are affected by individual valuation (via dysfunction judgments) as well as by how the condition is causally intervened upon. While physical dysfunctions are also viewed in a nonevaluative way, the lay understanding of mental dysfunction appears to be at least in part evaluative, depending on whether the condition enhances or diminishes subjective well-being. These differences highlight the importance of separating discussions of mental and physical conditions in future work.

Third, the findings also indicate that it would be helpful to *distinguish various aspects of value-ladenness*. It has generally been assumed that value-ladenness pertains either to the values held by the individual experiencing the condition or to the societal values prevailing in the individual's environment. Thus, to the extent that valuations matter for health and disease, much depends on whether or not the individual or society dislikes or perceives something as harmful. However, focusing solely on this aspect fails to uncover all the significant ways in which the relevant concepts can have an intimate connection to values. For example, evaluations of moral character appear to shape judgments about disease and disorder, irrespectively of whether the condition is mental or somatic. According to the pathologization hypothesis, negative moral evaluations of an individual increase the likelihood of classifying their condition as a disease while decreasing the likelihood of perceiving it as healthy, whether at a personal or subpersonal level. Furthermore, people vary in their right to moral evaluations in the context of healthcare, with doctors having greater moral standing than friends. It is crucial to broaden the scope of inquiry and differentiate between the effects of various types of valuations.

4.3 New (Explanatory) Tasks and Ethical Implications

We also propose that XPhiMed can reorient the debate by opening avenues for new tasks.[5] Loosely building on distinctions drawn by Stoljar (2017), we distinguish *boundary problems* (e.g., *where* is the line between what counts as health and as disease?) from *explanatory problems* (e.g., *why* do we classify certain things as diseases or health states?). To date, the philosophy of medicine literature has primarily focused on the former, and many of the studies reported in this Element illustrate how XPhiMed can make a valuable contribution to boundary problems. However, XPhiMed not only maps out the boundaries of these concepts, but, by exploring their broader "conceptual ecology," it can also shed light on the explanatory problem of *why* we classify certain conditions as diseases or as healthy.

How? XPhiMed can answer the *why* question by revealing the factors that drive the application of concepts, such as the concepts of dysfunction, valuation, and social vs. genetic cause. By identifying these factors, XPhiMed takes a crucial step toward understanding why and how we use these concepts, shedding light on the roles they purportedly play. A further task is to articulate these roles clearly and to explain, if multiple concepts of health and disease coexist, how they meet the diverse theoretical and practical demands arising across different contexts and demographic groups. Attaining greater clarity about these roles might reveal some

---

[5] Of course, new tasks may also include examining other health-related concepts such as distress or death through the lens of X-Phi.

potential ethical concerns with both lay and professional concepts that might call for revision (or even elimination). A couple of examples can serve for illustrative purposes.

First, if lifestyle is a dominant part of the cluster of properties associated with the concept of health, then this concept might result in expanding the domain of medical authority (a phenomenon we have called "medicalization") and a marginalization of segments of the population whose habits and activities do not fit those currently associated with a "healthy lifestyle." Framing diet, exercise, or sleep as medical concerns is likely to heighten societal pressure to conform to the associated behaviors as medical norms. It is not difficult to see how this could align with the existing trend of shifting responsibility for health outcomes disproportionately onto individuals, downplaying the role of social determinants of health such as lack of education, stigma, or economic inequality. These problematic effects will likely be even more pronounced if lifestyle is also a dominant part of the concept of health as understood by medical professionals, a topic for future research.

Second, while the findings reported in this Element suggest that at least some people mean something like the absence of disease by "health," future research should investigate why this is the case. Qualitative studies have indicated that individuals with lower socioeconomic status are more likely to embrace a negative conception of health, while in some studies at least those with higher socioeconomic status appear to give more weight to lifestyle characteristics. If future studies confirm this, this demographic variation might raise ethical concerns about a concept of health centered around lifestyle and likely warrant a call for revision.

Third, while we have noted that the pathologization effect should be considered separately from other types of valuation, it is essential to investigate this matter further at least along two lines. First, does the effect extend to medical professionals? We noted that if it does, medical professionals may be more likely to treat some phenotype common among a group as a disease if they hold negative evaluations about the relevant group. Second, we should also investigate whether there is a *reverse pathologization effect*, where unhealthy individuals or those with a disease are perceived as having worse moral character. Obesity might serve as a compelling test case, as it is viewed by some as a disease and by others as a natural variation. The inclination to classify obesity as a disease may, in part, stem from negative moral judgments about overweight individuals, highlighting the need to understand how moral evaluations influence disease classification.

4.4 Final Note

XPhiMed is still an emerging field, and in many ways, we have only just begun to explore its potential. Therefore, recognizing the preliminary nature of our work and the complexity of the issues at hand, we aimed to maintain a sense of humility in drawing conclusions. That said, XPhiMed does offer a new toolkit and does open new research avenues. If we have convinced you that this is the case, then our work was successful.

As our final note, while we do not expect everyone to fully appreciate or embrace this approach, we emphasize once again that our approach is *ecumenical* and that we are not in the business of declaring winners and losers among the positions explored in the literature. We hope it has become clear that, whether one adopts a restricted or unrestricted descriptive approach or advocates for developing new conceptual frameworks for health and disease, XPhiMed has the potential to serve as a valuable resource. We also maintain – and have argued – that regardless of the approach taken, XPhiMed provides insights that no perspective can afford to ignore.

Bibliography

Amoretti, M. C., & Lalumera, E. (2022). Wherein is the concept of disease normative? From weak normativity to value-conscious naturalism. *Medicine, Health Care and Philosophy, 25*(1), 47–60.

Ananth, M. (2008). *In defense of an evolutionary concept of health: Nature, norms, and human biology*. Ashgate Publishing Group.

Barnes, E. (2023). *Health problems: Philosophical puzzles about the nature of health*. Oxford University Press.

Beaulac, J., Kristjansson, E., & Cummins, S. (2009). A systematic review of food deserts, 1966–2007. *Preventing Chronic Disease, 6*(3), A105.

Béghin, G., & Faucher, L. (2023). Does the lay concept of mental disorder necessitate a dysfunction?. In K. Hens & A. de Block (Eds.), *Advances in experimental philosophy of medicine* (pp. 71–96). Bloomsbury.

Bishop, F., & Yardley, L. (2010). The development and initial validation of a new measure of lay definitions of health: The wellness beliefs scale. *Psychology and Health, 25*(3), 271–287.

Blaxter, M. (1990). *Health and lifestyles*. Routledge.

Blaxter, M. (2010). *Health*. Polity.

Boorse, C. (1975). On the distinction between disease and illness. *Philosophy and Public Affairs, 5*, 49–68.

Boorse, C. (1976). What a theory of mental health should be. *Journal for the Theory of Social Behavior, 6*, 61–84.

Boorse, C. (1977). Health as a theoretical concept. *Philosophy of Science, 44*, 542–573.

Boorse, C. (1997). A rebuttal on health. In J. M. Humber & R. F. Almeder (Eds.), *What is disease?* (pp. 3–143). Humana Press.

Boorse, C. (2011). Concepts of health and disease. In *Philosophy of medicine* (pp. 13–64). North-Holland.

Boorse, C. (2014). A second rebuttal on health. *Journal of Medicine and Philosophy, 39*(6), 683–724.

Braddon-Mitchell, D., Latham, A. J., & Varga, S. (ms). Is there a "folk" concept of dysfunction?

Broadbent, A. (2019). Health as a secondary property. *The British Journal for the Philosophy of Science, 70*, 609–627.

Burgess, A., & Plunkett, D. (2013a). Conceptual ethics I. *Philosophy Compass, 8*(12), 1091–1101.

Burgess, A., & Plunkett, D. (2013b). Conceptual ethics II. *Philosophy Compass, 8*(12), 1102–1110.

Bushnell, F. K. L., Cook, T. H., Wells, N., & Johnson, R. (2000). The meaning of health to the low-income patients in a primary care center. *Journal of Health Care for the Poor and Underserved, 11*(3), 267–275.

Buts, J., Baker, M., Luz, S., & Engebretsen, E. (2021). Epistemologies of evidence-based medicine: A plea for corpus-based conceptual research in the medical humanities. *Medicine, Health Care and Philosophy, 24*(4), 621–632.

Calnan, M. (1987). *Health and illness: The lay perspective*. Tavistock Publications.

Calnan, M., & Johnson, B. (1985). Health, health risks and inequalities: An exploratory study of women's perceptions. *Sociology of Health & Illness, 7*(1), 55–75.

Campbell, E. J. M., Scadding, J. G., & Roberts, R. S. (1979). The concept of disease. *British Medical Journal, 2*(6193), 757–762.

Canguilhem, G. (1966). *Le Normal et le pathologique*. Presses Universitaires de France.

Cappelen, H. (2018). *Fixing language: An essay on conceptual engineering*. Oxford University Press.

Carel, H. (2007). Can I be ill and happy?. *Philosophia, 35*(2), 95–110.

Carel, H. (2008). *Illness: The cry of the flesh*. Acumen.

Carnap, R. (1962). *Logical foundations of probability* (2nd ed.). The University of Chicago Press.

Centers for Disease Control and Prevention. (2020). Disability and health information for people with disabilities, at: www.cdc.gov/ncbddd/disabilityandhealth/people.html

Chalmers, D. J. (2015). Why isn't there more progress in philosophy? *Philosophy, 90*(1), 3–31.

Chalmers, D. J. (2020). What is conceptual engineering and what should it be? *Inquiry, 68*(9), 2902–2919.

Christie, J. R., Wilkinson, Z., Gawronski, S. A., & Griffiths, P. E. (2023). Concepts of function in biology and biomedicine. In K. Hens & A. De Block (Eds.), *Advances in experimental philosophy of medicine* (pp. 31–50). Bloomsbury.

Cooper, R. (2002). Disease. *Studies in History and Philosophy of Science Part C: Studies in History and Philosophy of Biological and Biomedical Sciences, 33*(2), 263–282.

Cooper, R. (2005). *Classifying madness*. Springer.

Cooper, R. (2016). Health and disease. In J. Marcum (Ed.), *The Bloomsbury companion to contemporary philosophy of medicine* (pp. 275–296). Bloomsbury.

Cooper, R. (2020). The concept of disorder revisited: Robustly value-laden despite change. In *Aristotelian Society Supplementary Volume* (Vol. 94, No. 1, pp. 141–161). Oxford University Press.

Cushman, F., & Mele, A. (2008). Intentional action: Two-and-a-half folk concepts? In J. Knobe & S. Nichols (Eds.), *Experimental philosophy* (pp. 171–188). Oxford University Press.

d'Houtaud, A., & Field, M. G. (1984). The image of health: Variations in perception by social class in a French population. *Sociology of Health and Illness*, 6(1), 30–60.

De Block, A., Dewitte, S., & Hens, K. (2023). Causes or cures: What makes us think of attention issues as disorders? *New Ideas in Psychology*, 69, article 101008.

De Block, A., & Hens, K. (2021). A plea for an experimental philosophy of medicine. *Theoretical Medicine and Bioethics*, 42(3–4), 81–89.

De Block, A., & Hens, K. (2023). Introduction: Whither (experimental) philosophy of medicine?. In Hens Kristien & de Block Andreas (Eds.), *Advances in experimental philosophy of medicine* (pp. 1–10). Bloomsbury.

De Block, A., & Sholl, J. (2021). Harmless dysfunctions and the problem of normal variation. In L. Faucher & D. Forest (Eds.), *Defining mental disorder: Jerome Wakefield and his critics* (pp. 495–510). The MIT Press.

De Jong, M. A., Wagemakers, A., & Koelen, M. A. (2020). "We Don't assume that everyone has the same idea about health, do we?" Explorative study of citizens' perceptions of health and participation to improve their health in a low socioeconomic city district. *International Journal of Environmental Research and Public Health*, 17(14), 4958.

De Vreese, L. (2017). How to proceed in the disease concept debate? A pragmatic approach. *The Journal of Medicine and Philosophy*, 42(4), 424–446.

DeVito, S. (2000). On the value-neutrality of the concepts of health and disease: Unto the breach again. *The Journal of Medicine and Philosophy*, 25(5), 539–567.

Dohle, S., Schreiber, M., Wingen, T., & Baumann, M. (2022). Blaming others for their illness: The influence of health-related implicit theories on blame and social support. *Journal of Applied Social Psychology*, 52(4), 210–219.

Downey, C. A., & Chang, E. C. (2013). Assessment of everyday beliefs about health: The lay concepts of health inventory, college student version. *Psychology and Health*, 28(7), 818–832.

Engelhardt Jr, H. T. (1976). Ideology and etiology. *Journal of Medicine and Philosophy*, *1*(3), 256–268.

Ereshefsky, M. (2009). Defining 'health' and 'disease'. *Studies in History and Philosophy of Science Part C: Studies in History and Philosophy of Biological and Biomedical Sciences*, *40*(3), 221–227.

Fagerberg, H. (2023). What we argue about when we argue about disease. *Philosophy of Medicine*, *4*(1), 1–9.

Faucher, L. (2021). Facts, facts, facts: HD analysis goes factual. In L. Faucher & D. Forest (Eds.), *Defining mental disorders: Jerome Wakefield and his critics* (pp. 47–70). The MIT Press.

Faucher, L., & Béghin, G. (2023). Experimental philosophy of psychiatry: A survey. In K. Hens & A. de Block (Eds.), *Advances in experimental philosophy of medicine* (pp. 11–30). Bloomsbury.

Favela, L. H., & Machery, E. (2023). Investigating the concept of representation in the neural and psychological sciences. *Frontiers in Psychology*, *14*, 1165622.

Feltz, A., & Cova, F. (2014). Moral responsibility and free will: A meta-analysis. *Conscious and Cognition*, *30*, 234–246.

Fugelli, P., & Ingstad, B. (2001). Health-people's perspective. *Tidsskrift for den Norske laegeforening: tidsskrift for praktisk medicin, ny raekke*, *121*(30), 3600–3604.

Fulford, K. W. M. (1989). *Moral theory and medical practice*. Cambridge University Press.

Fulford, K. W. M. (1999). Nine variations and a coda on the theme of an evolutionary definition of dysfunction. *Journal of Abnormal Psychology*, *108*, 412–420.

Fulford, K. W. M., & Colombo, A. (2004). Six models of mental disorder: A study combining linguistic-analytic and empirical methods. *Philosophy, Psychiatry, & Psychology*, *11*(2), 129–144.

Fulford, K. W. M., & Thornton, T. (2007). Fanatical about "harmful dysfunction". *World Psychiatry*, *6*(3), 161.

Fuller, J. (2018). What are chronic diseases? *Synthese*, *196*(7), 3197–3220.

Gagné-Julien, A. M. (2021). Dysfunction and the definition of mental disorder in the DSM. *Philosophy, Psychiatry, and Psychology*, *28*, 353–370.

Gagné-Julien, A. M. (2024). Beyond conceptual analysis: Social objectivity and conceptual engineering to define disease. *The Journal of Medicine and Philosophy: A Forum for Bioethics and Philosophy of Medicine*, *49*(2), 147–159.

Garson, J. (2019). *What biological functions are and why they matter*. Cambridge University Press.

Garson, J., & Piccinini, G. (2014). Functions must be performed at appropriate rates in appropriate situations. *British Journal for the Philosophy of Science 65*(1), 1–20.

Giroux, E. (2016). Introduction. Why a book on naturalism in the philosophy of health?. In E. Giroux (Ed.), *Naturalism in the philosophy of health: Issues and implications* (pp. 1–18). Springer International Publishing.

Goldman, A. I. (2007). Philosophical intuitions: Their target, their source, and their epistemic status. *Grazer Philosophische Studien, 74*(1), 1–26.

Goosens, W. K. (1980). Values, health, and medicine. *Philosophy of Science, 47*(1), 100–115.

Graham, G. (2010). *The disordered mind: An introduction to philosophy of mind and mental illness.* Routledge.

Griffiths, P. E., & Matthewson, J. (2018). Evolution, dysfunction, and disease: A reappraisal. *The British Journal for the Philosophy of Science, 69*, 301–327.

Griffiths, P. E., & Stotz, K. (2008). Experimental philosophy of science. *Philosophy Compass, 3*(3), 507–521.

Griffiths, P. E., Machery, E., & Linquist, S. (2009). The vernacular concept of innateness. *Mind and Language, 24*(5), 605–630.

Guerrero, J. D. (2010). On a naturalist theory of health: A critique. *Studies in History and Philosophy of Science Part C: Studies in History and Philosophy of Biological and Biomedical Sciences, 41*(3), 272–278.

Gunderman, R. (2000). Illness as failure: Blaming patients. *Hastings Center Report, 30*, 7–11.

Hausman, D. M. (2012). Health, naturalism and functional efficiency. *Philosophy of Science, 79*, 519–541.

Hausman, D. M. (2014). Health and functional efficiency. *The Journal of Medicine and Philosophy: A Forum for Bioethics and Philosophy of Medicine, 39*(6), 634–647.

Hausman, D. M. (2015). *Valuing health: Well-being, freedom and suffering.* Oxford University Press.

Hens, K., & de Block, A. (2023). Introduction: Whither (Experimental) philosophy of medicine?. In K. Hens & A. de Block (Eds.), *Advances in experimental philosophy of medicine* (pp. 1–10). Bloomsbury.

Herzlich, C. (1973). *Health and illness.* Academic Press.

Hesslow, G. (1993). Do we need a concept of disease?. *Theoretical Medicine, 14*, 1–14.

Hiscock, R., Bauld, L., Amos, A., Fidler, J. A., & Munafò, M. (2012). Socioeconomic status and smoking: A review. *Annals of the New York Academy of Sciences, 1248*, 107–123.

Huber, M., Knottnerus, J. A., Green, L., Van Der Horst, H., Jadad, A. R., Kromhout, D., Leonard, B., Lorig, K., Loureiro, M. I., van der Meer, J. W. M., Schnabel, P., Smith, R., van Weel, C., & Smid, H. (2011). How should we define health?. *Bmj, 343*.

Huber, M., van Vliet, M., Giezenberg, M., Winkens, B., Heerkens, Y., Dagnelie, P. C., & Knottnerus, J. A. (2016). Towards a 'patient-centred'operationalisation of the new dynamic concept of health: A mixed methods study. *BMJ Open, 6*(1), e010091.

Hughner, R. S., & Kleine, S. S. (2004). Views of health in the lay sector: A compilation and review of how individuals think about health. *Health, 8*(4), 395–422.

Katz, J., & Fodor, J. (1962). What's wrong with the philosophy of language?. *Inquiry, 5*(1–4), 197–237.

Kelley, M. (2005). Limits on patient responsibility. *The Journal of Medicine and Philosophy, 30*(2), 189–206.

Kingma, E. (2007). What is it to be healthy? *Analysis, 67*, 128–133.

Kingma, E. (2010). Paracetamol, poison and polio: Why Boorse's account of function fails to distinguish health and disease. *British Journal for the Philosophy of Science, 61*, 241–264.

Kingma, E. (2014). Naturalism about health and disease: Adding nuance for progress. *The Journal of Medicine and Philosophy, 39*(6), 590–608.

Kingma, E. (2017). Health, disease and naturalism: Hausman on the public value of health. *Public Health Ethics, 10*(2), 109–121.

Kingma, E. (2019). Contemporary accounts of health. In P. Adamson (Ed.), *Health: A history* (pp. 289–318). Oxford University Press.

Kirk, S. A., Wakefield, J. C., Hsieh, D., & Pottick, K. (1999). Social context and social workers' judgment of mental disorder. *Social Service Review, 73*(1), 82–104.

Knobe, J. (2003). Intentional action and side effects in ordinary language. *Analysis, 63*(3), 190–194.

Knobe, J., Buckwalter, W., Nichols, S., Robbins, P., Sarkissian, H., & Sommers, T. (2012). Experimental philosophy. *Annual Review of Psychology, 63*(1), 81–99.

Kohne, A. C. J., de Graauw, L. P., der Maas, R. L., & Os, J. V. (2023). Clinician and patient perspectives on the ontology of mental disorder: A qualitative study. *Frontiers in Psychiatry, 14*, 1081925.

Kornmesser, S., Bauer, A. M., Alfano, M., Allard, A., Baumgartner, L., Cova, F., Engelhardt, P., Fischer, E., Meyer, H., Reuter, K., Sytsma, J., Thompson, K., & Wyszynski, M. (2024). *Experimental philosophy for beginners: A gentle introduction to methods and tools*. Springer.

Kraaijeveld, S. R., & Jamrozik, E. (2022). Moralization and mismoralization in public health. *Medicine, Health Care and Philosophy*, *25*(4), 655–669.

Kukla, Q. R. (2014). Medicalization, "normal function," and the definition of health. In J. D. Arras, E. Fenton, and R. Kukla (eds.), *The Routledge companion to bioethics* (pp. 515–530). Routledge.

Kukla, Q. R. (2019). Infertility, epistemic risk, and disease definitions. *Synthese*, *196*(11), 4409–4428.

Kukla, Q. R. (2022). What counts as a disease, and why does it matter?. *The Journal of Philosophy of Disability*, *2*, 130–156.

Lalumera, E. (2025). Conceptual engineering of medical concepts. In M. G. Isaac, S. Koch, and K. Scharp (eds), *New perspectives on conceptual engineering-Volume 3: Applied Conceptual Engineering* (pp. 43–67). Springer Nature Switzerland.

Latham, A. J. (2019). The conceptual impossibility of free will error theory. *European Journal of Analytic Philosophy*, *15*(2), 99–120.

Lemoine, M. (2013). Defining disease beyond conceptual analysis: An analysis of conceptual analysis in philosophy of medicine. *Theoretical Medicine and Bioethics*, *34*, 309–325.

Lemoine, M., & Giroux, É. (2016). Is Boorse's biostatistical theory of health naturalistic?. In E. Giroux (Ed.). *Naturalism in the philosophy of health: Issues and implications* (pp. 19–38). Springer.

Lemoine, M., & Okholm, S. (2023). What experimental philosophy of disease should and should not be. In K. Hens & A. de Block (Eds.), *Advances in experimental philosophy of medicine* (pp. 97–110). Bloomsbury.

Lippert-Rasmussen, K., Latham, A. J., & Varga, S. (2025). A matter of standing: Praise and blame with respect to health. *The Journal of Ethics*, *29*, 663–680.

Lippert-Rasmussen, K., Latham, A. J., & Varga, S. (ms). Risk, disease, and moral standing to praise and blame.

Lloyd, E. A. (2006). The case of the female orgasm: Bias in the science of evolution. In *The case of the female orgasm*. Harvard University Press.

Lorente-Rovira, E., Grasa, E., Ochoa, S., Corripio, I., Peláez, T., López-Carrillero, R., Morano-Guillen, M., Gutierrez-Gea, A., Villagran, J. M., Llacer, B. & Sanjuán, J. (2020). Positive and useful voices in patients with schizophrenia: Prevalence, course, characteristics, and correlates. *The Journal of Nervous and Mental Disease*, *208*(8), 587–592.

Machery, E. (2009). *Doing without concepts*. Oxford University Press.

Machery, E. (2016). Experimental philosophy of science. In J. Sytsma & W. Buckwalter (Eds.), *A companion to experimental philosophy* (pp. 473–490). Blackwell.

Machery, E. (2017). *Philosophy within its proper bounds*. Oxford University Press.

Machery, E. (2023). The folk concept of disease. In K. Hens & A. de Block (Eds.), *Advances in experimental philosophy of medicine* (pp. 51–70). Bloomsbury.

Machery, E. (2025). A new challenge to conceptual engineering. *Inquiry*, 68(9), 3019–3042.

Machery, E., Griffiths, P., Linquist, S., & Stotz, K. (2019). Scientists' concepts of innateness: Evolution or attraction. In D. Wilkenfeld & R. Samuels (Eds.), *Advances in experimental philosophy of science* (pp. 172–201). Bloomsbury.

Machery, E., Mallon, R., Nichols, S., & Stich, S. P. (2004). Semantics, cross-cultural style. *Cognition*, 92(3), B1–B12.

Manne, K. (2025). *Unshrinking: How to face fatphobia*. Random House.

Matthewson, J., & Griffiths, P. E. (2017). Biological criteria of disease: Four ways of going wrong. *Journal of Medicine and Philosophy*, 42(4), 447–466.

Millstein, S. G., & Irwin, C. E. (1987). Concepts of health and illness: Different constructs or variations on a theme?. *Health Psychology*, 6(6), 515.

Mitchell, P., & Alexandrova, A. (2021). Well-being and pluralism. *Journal of Happiness Studies*, 22(6), 2411–2433.

Muckler, D., & Taylor, J. S. (2020). The irrelevance of harm for a theory of disease. *The Journal of Medicine and Philosophy*, 45(3), 332–349.

Murphy, D. (2006). *Psychiatry in the scientific image*. MIT Press.

Murphy, D. (2021). Concepts of disease and health. In Edward N. Zalta (Ed.), *The Stanford encyclopedia of philosophy* (Spring 2021 Edition). https://plato.stanford.edu/archives/spr2021/entries/health-disease/.

Nadelhoffer, T., Rose, D., Buckwalter, W., & Nichols, S. (2020). Natural compatibilism, indeterminism, and intrusive metaphysics. *Cognitive Science*, 44(8), e12873.

Nado, J. (2021). Conceptual engineering via experimental philosophy. *Inquiry*, 64(1–2), 76–96.

Nichols, S., & Knobe, J. (2007). Moral responsibility and determinism: The cognitive science of folk intuitions. *Nous*, 41(4), 663–685.

Nordenfelt, L. (1995). *On the nature of health: An action-theoretic approach*. Springer Science and Business Media.

Nordenfelt, L. (1998). On medicine and health enhancement-towards a conceptual framework. *Medicine, Health Care and Philosophy, 1*(1), 51–52.

Nordenfelt, L. (2001). On the goals of medicine, health enhancement and social welfare. *Health Care Analysis, 9*, 15–23.

Nordenfelt, L. (2007). The concepts of health and illness revisited. *Medicine, Health Care and Philosophy, 10*, 5–10.

Nordenfelt, L. (2017). On concepts of positive health. In T. Schramme & S. Edwards (Eds.), *Handbook of the philosophy of medicine* (pp. 29–43). Springer.

Peersman, W., Cambier, D., De Maeseneer, J., & Willems, S. (2012). Gender, educational and age differences in meanings that underlie global self-rated health. *International Journal of Public Health, 57*(3), 513–523.

Pottick, K. J., Wakefield, J., Kirk, S., & Tian, X. (2003). Influence of social workers' characteristics on the perception of mental disorder in youths. *Social Service Review, 77*(3), 431–454.

Reuter, K., Latham, A. J., & Varga, S. (2025). Concept(s) of health: Lifestyle at the heart of modern health. *Erkenntnis*, 1–26.

Reznek, L. (1987). *The nature of disease*. Routledge & Kegan.

Richardson, H. S. (2016). Capabilities and the definition of health: Comments on Venkatapuram. *Bioethics, 30*(1), 1–7.

Ringel, M. M., & Ditto, P. H. (2019). The moralization of obesity. *Social Science and Medicine, 237*, 112399.

Schramme, T. (2007). Lennart Nordenfelt's theory of health: Introduction to the theme. *Medicine, Health Care, and Philosophy, 10*(1), 3.

Schramme, T. (2017). Health as notion in public health. In T. Schramme & S. Edwards (Eds.), *Handbook of the philosophy of medicine*. Springer.

Schramme, T. (2023). Health as complete well-being: The WHO definition and beyond. *Public Health Ethics, 16*(3), 210–218.

Schupbach, J. N. (2017). Experimental explication. *Philosophy and Phenomenological Research, 94*(3), 672–710.

Schwartz, P. H. (2007a). Decision and discovery in defining 'disease'. In H. Kincaid & J. McKitrick (Eds.), *Establishing medical reality: Essays in the metaphysics and epistemology of biomedical science* (pp. 47–63). Springer.

Schwartz, P. H. (2007b). Defining dysfunction: Natural selection, design, and drawing a line. *Philosophy of Science, 74*(3), 364–385.

Schwartz, P. H. (2014). Reframing the disease debate and defending the biostatistical theory. *Journal of Medicine and Philosophy, 39*(6), 572–589.

Schwartz, P. H. (2017). Progress in defining disease: Improved approaches and increased impact. *Journal of Medicine and Philosophy*, *42*, 485–502.

Sholl, J. (2015). Escaping the conceptual analysis Straitjacket: Pathological mechanisms and Canguilhem's biological philosophy. *Perspectives in Biology and Medicine*, *58*, 395–418.

Sholl, J., & Rattan, S. I. (2020). How is 'Health' explained across the sciences? conclusions and recapitulation. In J. Sholl & S. I. Ratten (Eds.), *Explaining health across the sciences* (pp. 541–549). Springer.

Simon, J. G. (2007). Beyond naturalism and normativism: Reconceiving the 'disease' debate. *Philosophical Papers*, *36*(3), 343–370.

Simon, J. G., De Boer, J. B., Joung, I. M., Bosma, H., & Mackenbach, J. P. (2005). How is your health in general? A qualitative study on self-assessed health. *The European Journal of Public Health*, *15*(2), 200–208.

Smart, B. (2016). *Concepts and causes in the philosophy of disease*. Palgrave Macmillan.

Stegenga, J. (2018). *Medical nihilism*. Oxford University Press.

Steiner, P. M., Atzmüller, C., & Su, D. (2016). Designing valid and reliable vignette experiments for survey research: A case study on the fair gender income gap. *Journal of Methods and Measurement in the Social Sciences*, *7*(2), 52–94.

Stich, S. P., & Machery, E. (2023). Demographic differences in philosophical intuition: A reply to Joshua Knobe. *Review of Philosophy and Psychology*, *14*(2), 401–434.

Stoljar, D. (2017). *Philosophical progress: In defence of a reasonable optimism*. Oxford University Press.

Stotz, K., & Griffiths, P. (2004). Genes: Philosophical analyses put to the test. *History and Philosophy of the Life Science*, *26*(1), 5–28.

Stroebe, W. (2011). *Social psychology and health*. Open University Press.

Stronks, K., Hoeymans, N., Haverkamp, B., Den Hertog, F. R., van Bon-Martens, M. J., Galenkamp, H., Verwei, M., & Van Oers, H. A. (2018). Do conceptualisations of health differ across social strata? A concept mapping study among lay people. *BMJ Open*, *8*(4), e020210.

Sytsma, J., & Livengood, J. (2015). *The theory and practice of experimental philosophy*. Broadview Press.

Thorell, A. (2021). Distinguishing health from pathology. *The Journal of Medicine and Philosophy*, *46*(5), 561–585.

Thorell, A. (2024). Health and disease: Between naturalism and normativism. *Philosophy of Science*, *91*(2), 449–467.

Tse, J. S., & Haslam, N. (2023). What is a mental disorder? Evaluating the lay concept of mental ill health in the United States. *BMC Psychiatry*, *23*(1), 224.

van der Heijden, A., Te Molder, H., Jager, G., & Mulder, B. C. (2021). Healthy eating beliefs and the meaning of food in populations with a low socioeconomic position: A scoping review. *Appetite*, *161*, 105135.

van der Linden, R. R., & Schermer, M. H. (2024a). Exploring health and disease concepts in healthcare practice: An empirical philosophy of medicine study. *BMC Medical Ethics*, *25*(1), 38.

van der Linden, R. R., and Schermer, M. H. (2024b). Conceptual engineering health: A historical-philosophical analysis of the concept of positive health. In M. Schermer and N. Binney (Eds.), *A pragmatic approach to conceptualization of health and disease* (pp. 245–268). Springer.

van Heteren, F., Raaphorst, N., Groeneveld, S., & Bussemaker, J. (2023). Professionals' health conceptions of clients with psychosocial problems: An analysis based on an empirical exploration of semi-structured interviews. *International Journal of Nursing Studies Advances*, *5*, 100120.

Varga, S. (2020). Epistemic authority, philosophical explication, and the Bio-Statistical Theory of disease. *Erkenntnis*, *85*, 937–956.

Varga, S. (2024). *Science, medicine, and the aims of inquiry: A philosophical analysis*. Cambridge University Press.

Varga, S., & Latham, A. J. (2024a). Is health the absence of disease?. Inquiry 1–18.

Varga, S., & Latham, A. J. (2024b). What is mental health and disorder? Philosophical implications from lay judgments. Synthese.

Varga, S., & Latham, A. J. (2025). Is "Dysfunction" a value-neutral concept?. Philosophical Studies, 1–21.

Varga, S., Latham, A. J., & Machery, E. (2025a). The wicked and the Ill. Philosophical Psychology, 1–24.

Varga, S., Latham, A. J., & Machery, E. (2025b). "They Had It Coming!" The effect of moral character on somatic and mental health judgments. Royal Institute of Philosophy Supplements.

Varga, S., Latham, A. J., & Machery, E. (2025c). Concepts of health and disease: Insights from experimental philosophy of medicine. *Synthese*. 1–15 (Online First).

Varga, S., Latham, A. J., & Stegenga, J. (2025). Health, disease, and the medicalization of low sexual desire: A vignette-based experimental study. *ERGO*.

Varga, S., Andersen, M. M., Bueter, A., & Folker, A. P. (2024). Mental health promotion and the positive concept of health: Navigating dilemmas. *Studies in History and Philosophy of Science, 105*, 32–40.

Venkatapuram, S. (2011). *Health justice: An argument from the capabilities approach*. John Wiley & Sons.

Venkatapuram, S. (2013). Health, vital goals, and central human capabilities. *Bioethics, 27*(5), 271–279.

Wakefield, J. C. (1992a). The concept of mental disorder: On the boundary between biological facts and social values. *American Psychologist, 47*, 373–388.

Wakefield, J. C. (1992b). Disorder as harmful dysfunction: A concep-tual critique of DSM-HI-R's definition of mental disorder. *Psychological Review, 99*, 232–247.

Wakefield, J. C. (1999). Mental disorder as a black box essentialist concept. *Journal of Abnormal Psychology, 108*(3), 465–472.

Wakefield, J. C. (2005). On winking at the facts, and losing one's Hare: Value pluralism and the harmful dysfunction analysis. *World Psychiatry, 4*(2), 88–89.

Wakefield, J. C. (2007). The concept of mental disorder: Diagnostic implications of the harmful dysfunction analysis. *World Psychiatry, 6*(3), 149.

Wakefield, J. C. (2010). Taking disorder seriously: A critique of psychiatric criteria for mental disorders from the harmful-dysfunction perspective. In T. Millon, R. F. Krueger, & E. Simonsen (Eds.), *Contemporary directions in psychopathology: Scientific foundations of the DSM-V and ICD-11* (pp. 275–300). The Guilford Press.

Wakefield, J. C. (2021). Do the empirical facts support the harmful dysfunction analysis? Reply to Luc Faucher. In L. Faucher & D. Forest (Eds.), *Defining mental disorder: Jerome Wakefield and his critics* (pp. 71–96). MIT Press.

Wakefield, J. C., & Conrad, J. A. (2020). Harm as a necessary component of the concept of medical disorder: Reply to Muckler and Taylor. *The Journal of Medicine and Philosophy: A Forum for Bioethics and Philosophy of Medicine, 45*(3), 350–370.

Wakefield, J. C., Kirk, S., Pottick, K., & Hsieh, D. (1999). Disorder attribution and clinical judgment in the assessment of adolescent antisocial behavior. *Social Work Research, 23*(4), 227–238.

Wakefield, J. C., Kirk, S. A., Pottick, K. J., Tian, X., & Hsieh, D. K. (2006). The lay concept of conduct disorder: Do non-professional use syndromal symptoms or internal dysfunction to distinguish disorder from delinquency?. *Canadian Journal of Psychiatry, 51*(4), 210–217.

Walker, M. J., & Rogers, W. A. (2018). A new approach to defining disease. *Journal of Medicine and Philosophy*, *43*, 402–420.

Westerhof, G. J., & Keyes, C. L. M. (2010). Mental illness and mental health: The two continua model across the lifespan. *Journal of Adult Development*, *17*(2), 110–119.

Williams, R. (1983). Concepts of health: An analysis of lay logic. *Sociology*, *17*(2), 185–205.

World Health Organization. (1948). Summary Reports on Proceedings Minutes and Final Acts of the International Health Conference. https://apps.who.int/iris/handle/10665/85573

Wren-Lewis, S., & Alexandrova, A. (2021). Mental health without well-being. *The Journal of Medicine and Philosophy*, *46*(6), 684–703.

Artificial Intelligence Statement

One author (SV) used an AI-based language tool for language editing of parts of this Element and takes full responsibility for the content.

Cambridge Elements ≡

Philosophy of Biology

Grant Ramsey
KU Leuven

Grant Ramsey is a BOFZAP research professor at the Institute of Philosophy, KU Leuven, Belgium. His work centers on philosophical problems at the foundation of evolutionary biology. He has been awarded the Popper Prize twice for his work in this area. He also publishes in the philosophy of animal behavior, human nature, and the moral emotions. He runs the Ramsey Lab (theramseylab.org), a highly collaborative research group focused on issues in the philosophy of the life sciences.

About the Series

This Cambridge Elements series provides concise and structured introductions to all of the central topics in the philosophy of biology. Contributors to the series are cutting-edge researchers who offer balanced, comprehensive coverage of multiple perspectives, while also developing new ideas and arguments from a unique viewpoint.

Cambridge Elements=

Philosophy of Biology

Elements in the Series

Biological Organization
Leonardo Bich

Controlled Experiments
Jutta Schickore

Slime Mould and Philosophy
Matthew Sims

Explanation in Biology
Lauren N. Ross

Philosophy of Physiology
Maël Lemoine

The Organism
Jan Baedke

Human Cognitive Diversity
Ingo Brigandt

Modelling Evolution
Walter Veit

The Scope of Evolutionary Thinking
Thomas A. C. Reydon

What Is Life? Revisited
Daniel J. Nicholson

Biology and Medical Theory
Peter Takacs

Health and Disease: Experimental Philosophy of Medicine
Somogy Varga, Andrew J. Latham, and Edouard Machery

A full series listing is available at: www.cambridge.org/EPBY

For EU product safety concerns, contact us at Calle de José Abascal, 56–1°, 28003 Madrid, Spain or eugpsr@cambridge.org.